Key Stage 3
BITESIZE
revision

English

Imelda Pilgrim
Principal Examiner in GCSE English

and

Brian Conroy
Senior Examiner at KS3 and
Principal Examiner in GCSE English

BBC

Every effort has been made to contact copyright holders. The publishers would like to thank the following for permission to reproduce text:

Entry for 'good' – *Oxford Children's Thesaurus*, Oxford University Press.

'Blackberry-Picking' by Seamus Heaney, from *New Selected Poems* published by Faber & Faber.

Hens and Chicks – text and illustrations from *My Picture World Book of People, Places and Things* © 1990 Happy Books, Brown Watson, England.

'I Used to Live Here Once' by Jean Rhys from anthology *Sleep It Off Lady*, first published by Andre Deutsch, 1976.

Leaflet, 'Respect for Animals' by Respect for Animals.

'Beautiful Badgers' - Care for the Wild International, from *Wild About Animals* magazine, March/April 1998.

'The Lonely One' by Ray Bradbury from *Danger – The English Project Stage 2* published by Ward Lock International

Play the Game, Baseball, by Paul Gregory © Blandford 1993 Illustration © Ward Lock Ltd 1998 published by Blandford Press.

'Suncare for Schools' campaign – Health Education Authority

'Is Vivisection Right?' from *Bliss* magazine, April 1999

The Green Mamba – from *Going Solo* by Roald Dahl © Roald Dahl 1986 pub. Puffin Books

Published by BBC Educational Publishing
First published 1999
Reprinted in 2000
2nd reprint May 2000
© Imelda Pilgrim and Brian Conroy/ BBC Worldwide (Educational Publishing), 1999

Reproduced and printed in Great Britain by sterling.

Contents

Introduction

About Key Stage 3 Bitesize Revision

Key Stage 3 Bitesize Revision will help you do your best in your Key Stage 3 National Tests. It has many different elements to make an integrated learning package. The elements are:

KS3 Bitesize English: this book!
ISBN: 0 563 47432 7

TV programmes
(also available on video)
Video 1 ISBN: 0 563 47435 1
Video 2 ISBN: 0 563 47443 2

The website:
www.bbc.co.uk/education/ks3bitesize/
to get more practice in those areas
that you find difficult

REMEMBER The television programmes and website have cross-references to show where the book has more information on the subject. This book has TV and website symbols to show you where there is more information in the other parts of the Bitesize package. You can see the symbols on the page opposite.

This English book will help any of you who are hoping to achieve Levels 5, 6 and 7 in the Tests. Don't forget to use your notes from school and any textbooks you have been using for revision as well as the Bitesize materials.

The five Bitesize sections of this book each cover English topics that you will have been taught during Key Stage 3 (Years 7, 8 and 9).

Using the TV programmes and website

The Bitesize English TV programmes are broadcast in the middle of the night so you will have to record them on video. Remember to set the video the night before! KS3 Bitesize videos are also available to buy. Using the programmes on video means you can go back over the bits you're not sure of as many times as you like.

Have this Bitesize English book with you as you watch the videos. Don't try to watch a whole tape at once - watch one 'bite' and then work through that section in the book.

Key Stage 3 English

The National Curriculum programme of study for Key Stage 3 English is divided into four Attainment Targets. These are: English 1 - Speaking and Listening; English 2 - Reading; and English 3 - Writing.

The Key Stage 3 tests in English that you take near the end of Year 9 contain questions that cover English 2 and English 3. There are an equal number of marks available in all three parts of the Test. Everybody has to take the two Test papers. Paper 1 lasts for 1 hour 45 minutes, including 15 minutes' reading time. Paper 2 lasts for 1 hour 15 minutes.

Using this book to revise

- Plan your revision carefully. You'll take your Key Stage 3 English Tests in early May. Try to start your revision *at least* two months before you take your Tests to be sure you have enough time to cover all of the sections in this book. It's no good leaving your revision until the last moment.

- Break the subject up into bitesized chunks. That's why this book is divided into five short sections. You need to decide how many sections you must cover each week to get it all done before your Tests. Use the Contents page to plan your revision timetable. On your timetable, record your plan by writing the date you intend to work on each section alongside it.

- Try the quick questions (see the symbol at the bottom of this page) and the Test-style Practice questions in this book. There are suggested answers, where appropriate, on page 64.

- Plan the revision of all your Test subjects at the same time. Make sure you have breaks and time to relax; and organise your work around sports, hobbies and your favourite TV programmes!

Revision tips

You revise best when you are actively doing something.

- Write down important words and ideas as you work through each section.

- At the end of each section close the book and write down the key facts and ideas.

- For particular spellings and punctuation mistakes, 'Look, cover, write' and then 'check'.

- Practise using appropriate vocabulary.

- Write a set of summary notes for each section and rewrite them, in full, first copying the originals and then from memory.

- Test yourself by making flash cards. Write a key word on one side of a piece of card and the definition or explanation on the other.

- Revise with a friend - use the flash cards to test each other.

- Record your notes on to a cassette and make notes as you listen to it.

- Make a set of revision cards that fit into your pocket - test yourself on your way to school!

KEY TO SYMBOLS
📺 A link to the video

🔵 **On-line service.** You can find extra support, tips and answers to your exam queries on the Bitesize internet site. The address is http://www.bbc.co.uk/ education/revision

❓ Quick questions in this book for you to try as you go along.

 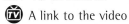

Reading non-fiction

At least one section of Paper One will ask you to look at non-fiction material. You have to give written answers to questions to show that you understand the purpose of the material.

⬛What is a non-fiction text?

Non-fiction writing is often used to give readers information, facts or advice that they might need. It may present a whole series of facts, as in a textbook. It can take the form of persuasive writing, encouraging the reader to do something, as in a charity or tourism leaflet. Sometimes non-fiction writing is used to present readers with an argument that influences or challenges their ideas. Non-fiction does not include imaginative storytelling, as fiction does.

What are non-fiction texts like?

The writing you'll be asked to look at in this section of the exam will probably be in one of these styles:

- a leaflet with words and pictures

- a piece of continuous prose writing.

Reading leaflets

Look at the advertisement for a schools campaign on sun safety on the page opposite. This is the sort of material you can expect to see in the KS3 National Test, if a leaflet is used in this section. You may be asked to write about how this leaflet persuades you to support the campaign. In this case, your answer needs to focus on <u>three</u> aspects: language, layout and pictures.

⬛ ⬛Language

Look for examples of words, phrases and sentences that persuade you to support the campaign, rather than just giving you factual information. You could use highlighter pens to help. Use one colour to highlight <u>facts</u> (information that is not in doubt and can be checked). In a different colour, highlight writing that isn't factual, but is working to gain your support. This type of writing may play upon your feelings. It may make you feel concerned, anxious or insecure.

Now look at the balance between the two types of writing (how much highlighter of each colour is there?). What does this tell you about the <u>purpose</u> of the leaflet?

❗ REMEMBER You must not simply describe the content of the leaflet.

❗ REMEMBER Some of the language in the leaflet is carefully chosen to affect your feelings.

SUNCARE FOR SCHOOLS CAMPAIGN 1999

sun know how

Dear Parent/Guardian,

The Health Education Authority (HEA) is committed to providing advice on sun safety to people of all ages. Children however are particularly vulnerable. On average 80% of a person's life time sun exposure occurs under the age of 18. It is a fact that sunburn during childhood greatly increases the risk of skin cancer in later life. It is important therefore that children are educated about the dangers of excessive sun exposure, but also provided by parents with the means to protect themselves.

The HEA's advice is simple:

Take care not to burn - *sunburn in childhood can lead to skin cancer in later life.*
Cover up *with cool, loose clothing, and hat and sunglasses.*
Seek shade *between 11am and 3pm - this is when the sun is strongest.*
Protect children - *particularly when they are too young to protect themselves.*
Use a sunscreen *SPF15 or above, apply generously and reapply frequently.*

Providing children with sunscreen is important as there are times when the sun is unavoidable. They are however expensive. The offer below does not come from the HEA.

Suncare for Schools is an independent non profit making organisation and although the HEA has no association or agreement of any kind with the Suncare for Schools, the HEA sees the merits in the offer and would urge you to seriously consider it. Please remember it is not the responsibility of teachers to apply sunscreen to children during school hours.

CHRIS NEW
Campaign Manager - Health Education Authority

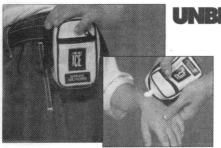

UNBEATABLE OFFER FOR PARENTS

70% OFF SPF 15 SUNCREAM AND SUNBLOCK

For £5.00 (including VAT and P&P) you can purchase 2 x 200ml of Hot Ice sunblock (SPF 30), **or** 2 x 200ml packs of Hot Ice SPF 15 suncream and receive a **FREE** orange nylon carry pouch that clips onto a belt loop or fastens directly onto a belt. - *it even has a zip pocket to carry money!*

Hot Ice suncream complies with EEC cosmetic regulations. The creams on offer have passed industry standard tests concerning SPF factors and UVA/UVB filter efficiency. Hot Ice does not contain animal fats, or nut preparations. It has been specially formulated for use on sensitive skin. It has not been tested on animals. For further details telephone 01604 781625.

Enjoy the sunshine but take care! In the short term sunburn is painful and unpleasant, but for the long term effects can be more serious.

- -

ORDER FORM   To be returned to school by **13th May 1999**

Please complete your child's details and fill in the total number of twin packs of Suncream you wish to order and the total amount of payment enclosed. The payment and this form should be returned to your school. Suncream will be delivered prior to the end of summer term.

Pupil's name: .... **Class:** ....

Please supply: [   ] (enter quantity) 2 x 200ml packs of Hot Ice SPF 15 sun cream with pouch priced at £5.00

[   ] (enter quantity) 2 x 200ml packs of Hot Ice Sunblock cream with pouch priced at £5.00

I enclose a payment for £_____ (enter amount). *Please make cheques payable to your school.*

📺 🔊 Format and layout

Another way in which people who produce leaflets try to get your support is through format and layout, or design. This leaflet would not attract readers if it was presented as a block of prose, like the page of a textbook. Instead it is designed in an eye-catching way. Look at the use of:

- headlines: important words in large writing attract the eye immediately

- signposts (for example, heavier type or sub-headings): these guide you through the leaflet so that you follow the order of information in the way the writer intends

- different styles of type: these make the leaflet varied and attractive.

How do the design aspects of this leaflet make it more <u>appealing</u>?

📺 🔊 Pictures

Look at the pictures used in the leaflet. Like the words, they are not just there to give you factual information. They reinforce the persuading work being done by the words.

Look at how the pictures are placed. They usually relate to and support the words in the writing that is next to them.

Sometimes a large, dramatic picture is used as a layout feature. It grabs your attention immediately and produces an instant reaction.

How does the content and placing of the pictures help to <u>persuade</u> you to give your support?

So, what have you learnt?

By working through these points in the leaflet, you have learnt:

- to see the difference between facts and other types of writing

- to understand how writers choose particular words and phrases to try and get your support

- to understand how important it is to break up the writing with features such as different kinds of typeface

- to understand how pictures relate to and support the words in the leaflet and can affect the layout

- to understand how all of the points listed above are deliberately used to persuade you to support the cause in the leaflet.

⊙⊙Reading prose

Another type of non-fiction writing may appear in this section of the exam. This type of writing will not include pictures or signposts, but it will still try to persuade you to agree with a particular point of view.

What will you be asked to do?

As with the previous type of non-fiction writing, you will need show the examiner that you can:

- be clear about the difference between fact and opinion

- follow the argument and ideas of the writer

- spot when the writer has deliberately chosen certain words and phrases to affect your feelings. For example, the writer may have used language in a particular way that makes you feel angry, sad or excited.

You will not be asked to look at layout, but you will need to understand why some information has been placed where it is in the article.

Read through the following extract. The author is writing about an unplanned visit he made to Durham. In it he tries to persuade the reader that Durham is a splendid city to visit.

Passage 1: Notes From a Small Island by Bill Bryson

I was heading for Newcastle, by way of York, when I did another impetuous thing. I got off at Durham, intending to poke around the cathedral for an hour or so and fell in love with it instantly in a serious way. Why, it's wonderful – a perfect little city – and I kept thinking: 'Why did no-one tell me about this?' I knew, of course, that it had a fine Norman cathedral but I had no idea that it was so *splendid*. I couldn't believe that not once in twenty years had anyone said to me, 'You've never been to Durham? Good God, man, you must go at once! Please – take my car.' I had read countless travel pieces in Sunday papers about weekends away in York, Canterbury, Norwich, even Lincoln, but I couldn't remember reading a single one about Durham, and when I asked friends about it, I found hardly any who had ever been there. So let me say it now: if you have never been to Durham, go at once. Take my car. It's wonderful.

The cathedral, a mountain of reddish-brown stone standing high above a lazy green loop of the River Wear, is, of course, its glory. Everything about it was perfect – not just its setting and execution but also, no less notably, the way it is run today. For a start there was no nagging for money, no 'voluntary' admission fee. Outside, there was simply a discreet sign announcing that it cost £700,000 a year to maintain the cathedral and that it was now engaged on a £400,000 renovation project on the east wing and that they would very much appreciate any spare money that visitors might give them. Inside, there were two modest collecting boxes and nothing else – no clutter, no nagging notices, no irksome bulletin boards or stupid Eisenhower flags, nothing at all to detract from the unutterable soaring majesty of the interior. It was a perfect day to see it. Sun slanted lavishly through the stained-glass windows, highlighting the stout pillars with their sumptuously grooved patterns and spattering the floors with motes of colour. There were even wooden pews.

I'm no judge of these things, but the window at the choir end looked to me at least the equal of the more famous one at York, and this one at least you could see in all its splendour since it wasn't tucked away in a transept. And the stained-glass window at the other end was even finer. Well, I can't talk about this without babbling because it was just so wonderful. As I stood there, one of only a dozen or so visitors, a verger passed and issued a cheery hello. I was charmed by this show of friendliness and captivated to find myself amid such perfection, and I unhesitatingly gave Durham my vote for best cathedral on planet Earth.

When I had drunk my fill, I showered the collection pot with coins and wandered off for the most fleeting of looks at the old quarter of town, which was no less ancient and beguiling, and returned to the station feeling simultaneously impressed and desolate at just how much there was to see in this little country and what folly it had been to suppose that I might see anything more than a fraction of it in seven flying weeks.

REMEMBER You must not merely describe the content of the article. Understanding the content is only a starting point.

(?) *Look carefully at the factual information in the article. You might like to highlight key words and phrases. Write a brief summary containing all the fact-based (as opposed to opinion-based) information.*

Use of language

In a different colour to the one you used in the exercise above, highlight the words and phrases the writer uses to help you understand how he sees Durham and its cathedral, for example: 'a perfect little city', 'splendid'.

You'll see that some examples (like 'in all its splendour') are quite clearly trying to persuade you. Others affect your feelings, (for example, 'no voluntary admission fee'), although it is more difficult to pinpoint what the effect is.

Using these highlighted words and phrases make a list of 'Persuasive language'.

REMEMBER
Use well-chosen examples when you write about language that affects your feelings. Say what those feelings are.

Persuasion and argument

Look at the order in which you are given information. See also if the language which affects your feelings becomes more powerful during the course of the extract. Why might the writer have chosen to give you these ideas in this particular order? For example, he moves from outlining the reason for his visit to a description of Durham cathedral and from there to a comparison with York.

Think about the previous section in which you considered how pictures are used in leaflets. They are deliberately placed to have a dramatic effect on the reader. In the extract above, the writer is doing the same thing in the way he orders his paragraphs. This setting-out, or structure, brings together different aspects of the writing to have an <u>impact</u> on the reader. It is working to <u>persuade</u> you of the writer's point of view, so that you <u>agree with his ideas</u>.

What do you know now?

You can now understand:

- how to extract factual information from a piece of writing

- how the use of language helps the writer to present ideas

- how the way in which the writer sets out the article helps him to persuade the reader

- how different factors work together to give the article impact and achieve its purpose.

Practice

Read through the extract on Bill Bryson's visit to Durham. In what ways does the writer try to persuade you that a visit to this city is a worthwhile experience?

Your answer should include comments on:

- the descriptive information the writer gives about Durham and its cathedral

- the ways in which the writer presents the evidence for a visit to Durham

- the effect of the last paragraph

- the extent to which the article persuades readers that a visit to Durham is an experience they should try.

Writing non-fiction

Every piece of writing has a <u>purpose</u> and an <u>audience</u>. The <u>purpose</u> of a piece of writing is the reason why it is being written. The <u>audience</u> of a piece of writing is the person or people who are intended to read it.

Identifying purpose and audience

Read this question from an exam paper:

Imagine you are a director of a new museum. (You can decide what is in the museum). Write a letter to headteachers of schools in the area encouraging them to bring groups of pupils to visit the museum.

REMEMBER
It is important to be clear about the purpose of your writing and the audience for whom you are writing before you start to write.

You are being asked to write a letter. The purpose of the letter is to persuade schools to bring groups of pupils to visit the museum. The audience of the letter is headteachers of local schools.

Now read questions A and B, below, and complete this chart:

Question	Purpose	Audience
A	To persuade others to support your view	
B		

A Imagine you have been given a chance to talk in your year assembly. Choose an issue you feel strongly about. Write a speech trying to persuade other people to support your views.

B A place that is important to you is under threat. This place could be a park, an interesting building or an area of the countryside. Write an article for local people explaining why this place should be kept as it is.

Matching writing to purpose and audience

Once you have identified your purpose and audience, you need to think about how you can match your writing to them in an appropriate way.

The following piece was written for young children (the audience) to tell them how chicks grow (the purpose).

When the chicks are fully formed, they use their little beaks to break open the eggshells.

The hen is keeping her eggs warm. Inside each egg a chick develops.

Some of the newly-hatched chicks will grow up to be cockerels and some will grow into hens.

The writer has matched his writing to the purpose and the audience by:

- using simple sentence structures
- using words that most young children can read
- closely linking sentences through ideas
- introducing only one new idea in each sentence
- using illustrations to break up the written text.

(?) *Write a short piece for young children in which you tell them how something is made. You do not need to include pictures, but do remember to:*
- *keep your sentences short and simple*
- *use words that young children will understand*
- *only introduce one idea at a time.*

One of the first things the examiner will look for is how well you match your writing to purpose and audience. If you don't give enough thought to this, you can get it very wrong.

Look again at the first question you were asked to consider on page 12. Remind yourself of its purpose and audience. Now read the beginning of a letter based on this task:

> Dear Head,
> I've got a new museum and it would be really great if you could get your kids to come here. There are loads of things for them to do. We've got a really good cafe where the kids can buy burgers and pizzas and there's a shop next to the museum which is really cheap.
> The museum's dead easy to get to from your school and you can find it on any map. Everyone who comes here thinks it's ace but if anyone does get bored they can mess about outside or visit the nearby amusement arcade.

First think about the purpose. What does this letter actually tell the headteacher about the museum? Is the information it gives helpful? What details might make the headteacher <u>not</u> want to visit the museum?

Now think about the audience. The writer uses a lot of slang, for example: 'really great', 'loads of'. How many other examples of slang can you find? Is this language appropriate to the audience?

! REMEMBER
It is important to match what you write and the way you write it to your purpose and audience.

Practice

Write your own letter in response to this question:

Your class has agreed to help a local children's hospital or home.
Write a letter to the parents of your year group explaining what you plan to do.

Making choices and organising ideas

 Part of the assessment of your writing in the exam is based on how good your ideas are and how well you organise them. In order to succeed in this you need to do a lot of thinking and planning before you start to write.

The first thing you need to do is to think hard about which of the writing tasks you can do best. Some candidates simply read the first question, decide they can do it and then start to write. They write for fifteen minutes and then run out of things to say. At this point, they either stop writing or add bits on that should have been written earlier. You need to use your time more carefully. You are advised to spend about thirty-five to forty minutes on the writing section. It's a good idea to spend about ten minutes of this time on thinking and planning.

Follow the stages below carefully.

1 Making a choice

REMEMBER
Choose your question carefully and gather and plan ideas before you start to write your response.

Read each of the questions carefully. Choose the one you find most interesting and that you know you can write about – there's no point choosing to write an article about wildlife, for example, if you don't know much about it.

Read your chosen task again. It may help you to underline or highlight certain words in the question. Make a note of the purpose, the audience and the form your writing is to take.

Example:

> A place that is important to you is under threat. This place could be a park, an interesting building or part of the countryside. Write an <u>article</u> for <u>local people</u> <u>explaining why</u> this place should be kept as it is.

Purpose: to explain why the place should be kept as it is.

Audience: local people.

Form: an article.

2 Gathering ideas

Once you have chosen your task, you need to get some ideas together. Many of the questions will give you some suggestions for the kinds of things you could write about.

Look at the example question again.

In your answer to this question you could include the following ideas:

- a description of the place

- why it is important to you

- reasons why it should be saved

- how other people could help you to save it.

This does not mean you have to write about these things, but it gives you a useful starting point. Another useful starting point is to ask yourself these questions: What? Where? When? Why? How?

You could choose to write your ideas down in the form of a 'brainstorm'. The more ideas you gather, the more interesting your letter will be.

! REMEMBER Brainstorming is when you write down all the ideas that occur to you about a subject, whether you use them in the end, or not.

3 Organising ideas

The next step is to organise your ideas. Decide which ideas fit together best and the order in which you want to write them. You need to decide on your paragraphs, so it is a good idea to make a brief plan. Here is an example of a paragraph plan for the example question:

Para. 1 – describe park – natural beauty – peaceful place in busy town
Para. 2 – importance to children – play area – nature studies – safe short-cut
Para. 3 – importance to elderly – meeting place – bowling green – café
Para. 4 – other uses – attracts visitors – place for outdoor concerts
Para. 5 – emphasise importance to the local community – encourage readers to sign petition and write to local councillors.

Once you have organised your ideas, you are ready to start writing

Thinking about words

 In your English Test, your examiner will assess your ability to:

■ use a varied vocabulary

■ use vocabulary effectively.

To show this, you need a wide range of words at your fingertips. You can then choose the most appropriate words in order to express your ideas effectively.

Making words work for you

Many students already know a wide range of words, but don't use these in their writing. They tend to stick to the words they have always used, instead of being a bit more adventurous. They still write with the same vocabulary they used in primary school, even though they now know many more words.

(?) *Read the two paragraphs below. One has been written using simple vocabulary. The other introduces a much wider range of words.*

A

I live in a small town near the seaside. It's a busy place and lots of things happen here. In the summer, when the weather is good, a lot of visitors come to my town. They get here by car but also by bus. When they get here they spend most of their time on the beach or in the shops.

B

I live in a small, picturesque town close to the coast. It's a busy, bustling place where many exciting events occur. In the height of summer, when the sun is blazing and the skies are blue, hordes of visitors descend on the town. They usually travel by car or by bus. When they arrive they tend to divide their time between the sandy beach and the colourful shops.

(?) *Highlight the differences in use of vocabulary by completing this chart. The first three have been done for you.*

A	B
a small town	a small, picturesque town
near the seaside	close to the coast
a busy place	a busy, bustling place
lots of things happen here	
In the summer	
when the weather is good	
a lot of visitors	
come to my town	
They get here by	
When they get here	
they spend most of their time	
the beach	
the shops	

(?) *Re-write the following paragraph using a wider and more interesting range of vocabulary:*

> The town was first built by the Romans because it was in a good place for trading. Its streets are not very wide. Some of the buildings are very old though there are a lot of new ones as well. One of the biggest buildings is the Town Hall which is near the train station. There is a stone cross in the middle of the town and this is a good place for meeting friends.

Increasing your range of words

One way of improving your writing is to use more of the words you already know; but it is also essential that you extend your range of words. One of the best ways of doing this is to use a thesaurus. This offers you a range of words that are similar, though not exactly the same, in meaning. As a word can have different meanings in different contexts, the thesaurus shows you the appropriate way in which to use the word.

Take, for example, the word 'good'. This is a word that is often over-used.

REMEMBER Always look at the correct context for a particular word in a thesaurus. The word may make no sense if you use it in the wrong place.

When you look up 'good' in a Thesaurus, you are given a range of words that can be used in its place:

> good 1 *a good deed, a good person.* admirable, appropriate, benevolent, caring, commendable, considerate, creditable, dutiful, esteemed, fair, great, helpful, holy, honest, honourable, humane, innocent, just, kind, kind-hearted, law-abiding, marvellous, moral, noble, obedient, outstanding, praiseworthy, proper, reliable, religious, right, righteous, saintly, thoughtful, upright, virtuous, well-behaved, wonderful, worthy. 2 *a good musician, a good worker.* able, accomplished, capable, clever, conscientious, creditable, efficient, (informal) fabulous, gifted, proficient, skilful, skilled, talented, thorough. 3 *a good holiday, good weather.* agreeable, delightful, enjoyable, excellent, fine, heavenly, lovely, nice, pleasant, pleasing, satisfactory, (informal) terrific.

(?) *Re-write these simple sentences, replacing the word 'good' with a different word:*

She was a good dancer.

The teacher said he was a good boy.

I had a good day in town.

She made a good choice for the school outing.

There are a number of other things you can do to increase your range of words:

■ always ask what a word means if you hear or see one you don't know

■ use a dictionary to help you find out the meanings of unfamiliar words

■ keep a list of any new words you come across and remind yourself of them regularly.

Using words effectively

For words to work effectively they need to target their purpose and audience. The extract opposite is taken from a leaflet about trapping and breeding animals for their fur. In it, the writer is trying to persuade the reader that this practice is wrong.

Many of the words used in this extract are intended to make the reader feel sorry for the animals and disturbed by their deaths. This use of language is called 'emotive', which means that it appeals directly to the reader's emotions.

'glamorous facade' - suggests that the glamour is only a pretence

'dies for "fashion"' - a play on the saying that something is 'to die for'

Every second an **animal dies** for 'fashion'

That is the appalling reality that lies behind the fur trade's glamorous facade. Every winter some **35 million** beautiful, intelligent mammals are killed just for the fur on their backs. That works out to the equivalent of **one animal for every second of every minute of every day of the year** dying often after suffering excruciating pain and unnecessary suffering.

During the time that it takes you to read this leaflet the fur trade will have caused a further 250 creatures to have perished.

'appalling' - stresses the awfulness of killing animals for fur

'beautiful, intelligent' - these words emphasise the animals' appeal

'every' - repeated to emphasise the numbers of animals that are dying

'excruciating' - illustrates how extreme the animals' pain is

'unnecessary' - suggests needless waste of life

Practice

Choose a subject you feel strongly about. Write a few paragraphs about it, in which you try to influence your reader's feelings by using language emotively.

Sentence structure and paragraphing

 It is not just the range of words you use that is important. In the Test your examiner will assess your ability to:

■ organise words into sentences

■ organise sentences into paragraphs.

Words into sentences

Almost all writing is organised in sentences. Words are placed in a particular sequence to communicate an idea, or several ideas, clearly to the reader. There are three main types of sentence.

<u>Simple sentences:</u> these communicate one idea.

For example: The shops were shut.

<u>Compound sentences:</u> these link two or more simple sentences by using conjunctions, words such as *and*, *but*, *so* and *or*.

For example: The shops were shut so we went to the cinema.

<u>Complex sentences:</u> these communicate more than one idea by using two or more clauses, usually separated by commas.

For example: As it was a Sunday, the shops were shut, so we went to the cinema.

Read the following extract, in which Bill Bryson writes about his American home town of Des Moines. The notes at the side will help you to identify the different types of sentence structure and to understand why the writer has chosen to use them.

Passage 1: The Lost Continent by Bill Bryson

> The extract starts with two very short, simple sentences. This is an effective way of starting a piece of writing, as it grabs the reader's attention and, in this case, emphasises the writer's feelings about his home town.

> This is a long, compound sentence which contains a lot of repetition of ideas. By using this particular sentence form and the repetition, Bryson emphasises the monotony of life in Des Moines.

I come from Des Moines. Somebody had to.

When you come from Des Moines you either accept the fact without question and settle down with a local girl named Bobbi and get a job at the Firestone factory and live there for ever and ever, or you spend your adolescence moaning at length about what a dump it is and how you can't wait to get out, and then you settle down with a local girl named Bobbi and get a job at the Firestone factory and live there for ever and ever.

Hardly anyone ever leaves. This is because Des Moines is the most powerful hypnotic known to man. Outside town there is a big sign that says WELCOME TO

DES MOINES. THIS IS WHAT DEATH IS LIKE. There isn't really. I just made that up. But the place does get a grip on you. People who have nothing to do with Des Moines drive in off the interstate, looking for gas or hamburgers, and stay for ever. There's a New Jersey couple up the street from my parents' house whom you see wandering around from time to time looking faintly puzzled but strangely serene. Everybody in Des Moines is strangely serene.

> In this complex sentence our attention is drawn to the ordinary reasons why some people first visited the town. This creates humour when the author goes on to say that they stayed on forever.

In your writing you should aim to use a variety of sentence structures.

(?) *Write a short introduction to your home town. Aim to use a range of sentence structures in your writing.*

Organising sentences into paragraphs

In writing, words are usually organised into sentences and sentences are usually organised into paragraphs. The paragraph is a visual sign to the reader that something new is being introduced.

There are two ways to show the reader where a new paragraph begins:

- by indenting the first word so that the paragraph starts a little way in from the margin
- by leaving a line between paragraphs.

Usually, when writing by hand, you indent the first word. Each paragraph has its own topic. The subject of the paragraph may link with that of the paragraphs before and after it, but it should be possible to identify a new and different subject or series of ideas within each paragraph.

Read the following text about baseball.

Passage 2: from Play the Game, Baseball by Paul Gregory

Baseball has retained its popularity in the face of strong competition from other sports, has continued to justify prime time television slots across North America, where it is at its strongest, and, in its variants, has become *the* ball game played by mixed groups the world over as an easily-staged, enjoyable and competitive social activity.

The professional game still draws big crowds to stadia throughout the United States and Canada almost every night of the week. The atmosphere of a live game attracts the supporters despite national TV coverage and the diverse sporting menu offered by the small screen. Star players are heroes, the leagues competitive, newcomers are microscopically studied and veterans of the game revered and adored.

At college and university level the game is professionally organised and enthusiastically sponsored with the media eager to chart the progress of young players through this 'feeder'

system. Earlier still, in the parks and yards, most American youngsters – and others around the world – take up a bat and ball at a very early age and start out in a sport which many stay with for life.

Like soccer, baseball and softball benefit from the minimal cost required to create a game. A basic baseball field can be marked out on almost any surface and spare area of ground; with bat, ball and players you are up and running. Once you have thrown your first pitch, struck your first run or taken a high catch, you will want to play again, and again.

These four paragraphs are part of an introduction to a book on baseball. In a logical order, they develop the idea that baseball is a popular sport and trace its international popularity back to its attraction to youngsters in the park.

Each paragraph deals with a slightly different aspect of the sport:

Para. 1 – the popularity of baseball worldwide

Para. 2 – the popularity of professional baseball

Para. 3 – the popularity of baseball at college level and earlier

Para. 4 – why baseball is so popular.

Notice how each paragraph links with the one that follows it, and how the ideas are placed in a logical order.

Practice

Choose a sport or hobby you are interested in and/or know something about. Write an introduction to it. Aim to write four paragraphs. Before you start to write, decide what each paragraph will be about and make a paragraph plan.

Writing in different forms

As you have seen in **'Reading non-fiction'**, there are many different kinds of non-fiction text. In your exam you are most likely to be asked to write one of the following:

- a letter
- an article
- a speech.

One of the things your examiner will look for is your ability to write in the appropriate form. There are certain features of these different forms that you need to be familiar with.

Writing a letter

There are two types of letter – formal and informal. It is most likely that you will be asked to write a formal letter. Look carefully at how your letter should be presented. The recipient is the person to whom you are writing.

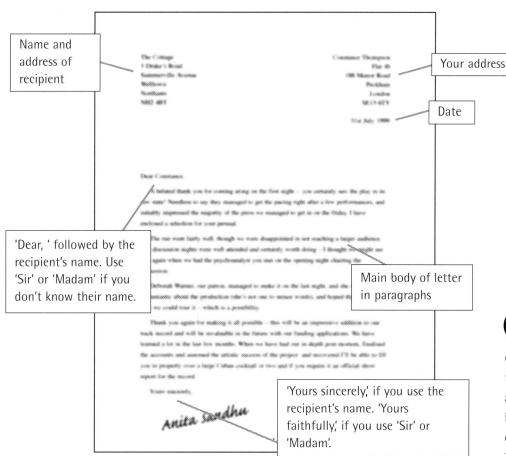

Name and address of recipient

Your address

Date

'Dear, ' followed by the recipient's name. Use 'Sir' or 'Madam' if you don't know their name.

Main body of letter in paragraphs

'Yours sincerely,' if you use the recipient's name. 'Yours faithfully,' if you use 'Sir' or 'Madam'.

This is the basis of how to set out a formal letter.

❗ REMEMBER
Sometimes in the exam you will be asked not to include the addresses. Follow the instructions you are given carefully.

Getting the layout right is only a small part of writing a good letter. It is what you say that is most important. You should aim to be clear and to the point. Read the following letter carefully. The notes next to it give you some useful clues on how to write a good letter.

– clear opening statement which identifies the issue

– written in the first person, using 'I' and 'we'

– in the present tense

– ideas organised into paragraphs

– development of ideas

– mix of factual detail and opinion

– use of rhetorical questions

– emphasis of aim at end

! **R E M E M B E R**
Rhetorical questions don't expect an answer. They are used to make the reader think and question.

Dear Councillor,

I am a thirteen-year-old living on Highfields Estate and I wish to complain about the lack of facilities for young people in our town.

Adults, including yourself, frequently complain about the behaviour and attitude of teenagers in our town but it seems to me that you do very little to help us. On my estate there is no youth club and nowhere for young people like me to go. Is it any wonder that so many young people tend to meet up at the local shops where, at least, there is some light and somewhere to sit? We like to relax, just as adults do, but we need a place where we can relax.

In Barton they look after their young people. There is a leisure centre with a brilliant swimming pool, a bowling alley with a cafe and pool tables, and I know of at least two youth clubs. It's too far away, however, for most of us to get to in the evenings and the last bus back is at 8.30. Why should the teenagers of Barton have so many facilities while we don't have any?

There are as many young people in this town as in Barton. Surely it is time that you and the other councillors thought about us and, instead of criticising, did something to help?

Yours sincerely,

Beth Pilgrim

Practice

Write a letter to a local councillor about the facilities for teenagers in your area. Aim to:
■ identify the main issue in your opening paragraph
■ write in the first person
■ use the present tense
■ develop your ideas
■ emphasise your main point at the end.

Writing an article

Articles most commonly appear in newspapers and magazines. They can be on almost any subject. Read this extract from an article on badgers:

BEAUTIFUL BADGERS

Where do badgers live?

Badgers live in social groups called clans, which contain related adults and their young. They tend to be peaceable and there is usually little aggression between clan members. Each clan has a territory which they will defend from intruders who are not part of the clan.

Badger cubs

Badger cubs are usually born between late December and early April. The cubs – usually two to three in a litter – remain below ground for the first eight to ten weeks, though they depend on their mother for a further two to three weeks while they learn to fend for themselves.

What do badgers eat?

About half of the badger's diet is earthworms and they can catch as many as 200 in a single night. Badgers also eat fruit, seeds, beetles, rabbits, hedgehogs and insects. Badgers are like the dustmen of the countryside, munching up almost anything they happen to come across.

Notice how this article is introduced with a heading which uses alliteration (Beautiful Badgers) to catch the reader's attention. The content is organised into paragraphs. Sub-headings are used to summarise the content of each section. Articles are usually written in the first person (I, we) or the third person (he, she, it, they). Which person is this article written in? The writer uses a lot of factual detail as well as some opinion. While many articles are printed in columns, you do not need to do this in your exam. It wastes time and gains you no marks.

 **REMEMBER**
Alliteration is when two or more words starting with the same letter or sound are put together deliberately for effect.

 Write a short article for an animal magazine about an animal you are interested in. Aim to:
- *choose an interesting heading*
- *organise your ideas, using sub-headings*
- *include relevant factual detail.*

Writing a speech

Speech writing is a very different form to letter or article writing. For a start, speeches are intended to be spoken, not read. There are a number of features commonly used in speeches. Read the following extracts from a very famous speech by Martin Luther King and the notes that accompany them:

Here Martin Luther King addresses his audience as his friends. He is speaking in the first person directly to them. He repeats the word 'dream' four times to emphasise it, because he wants his audience to share his dream.

'I say to you today, my friends . . .
I still have a dream. It is a dream deeply rooted in the American dream. I have a dream that one day this nation will rise up and live out the true meaning of its creed. We hold these truths to be self-evident that all men are created equal.

Again, Martin Luther King uses a lot of repetition. Think about the words he repeats and the reasons for this. The ellipsis (. . .) is a common form of punctuation used to show a pause or break. In this case, it is being used to show that the speaker is pausing for effect. The exclamation marks show that the words are spoken with particular force or emphasis.

'Let freedom ring . . !
Allow freedom to ring . . !
from every mountainside . . .
from every peak . . .
from every village and every hamlet . . .
we will be able to join hands and sing . . .
"Free at last, free at last;
thank God Almighty, we are free at last."'

Another common feature of speeches is the use of rhetorical questions. No answer is expected to these questions. They are used to make the listener think and question.

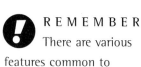 **REMEMBER**
There are various features common to letters, articles and speeches, for example: they are organised into paragraphs, they often use the present tense and may have rhetorical questions. Aim to use these features in your own writing.

 Write a speech to give to your class on a subject you feel strongly about. Aim to:
- *address your audience directly*
- *use repetition for effect*
- *use rhetorical questions*
- *use ellipsis (. . .) and exclamation marks (!) for force and impact.*

As with a letter and an article, it is the content of a speech that is most important.

Writing to argue

Some of the writing tasks in the Test may ask you to give your opinion on a particular issue or to explain the reasons why you feel strongly about something. In questions such as these, you are being asked to present and develop a particular point of view, in other words to build an argument. Your opinion may be based on personal experience or on evidence taken from other sources.

Read the following article, which contains contrasting responses to the same question:

Should animals be used in medical experiments?

Is **vivisection** right?

We asked Judith, an animal rights activist and Sarah, who has had part of her left leg amputated because of cancer, to give us their views on animal medical testing.

Judith Levitt, 21 from Sheffield, has been actively involved in animal rights since she was a teenager. She believes animals should not be tested on for science

"I became a vegetarian when I was 11, and as a teenager was involved with animal groups like the Vegetarian Society and the British Union for the Abolition of Vivisection. I went on about 15 demos, usually they were walks through London with about 15-20,000 people.

I've written to medical research organisations to get into labs and see how animals are treated during testing, but they've never let me in. I hate vivisection 'cause the animals aren't treated humanely.

I don't think the labs are honest with the public about the suffering the animals go through. There are countless examples of animal rights activists going into labs undercover and discovering horrific things. There are meant to be all sorts of regulations, like RSPCA inspectors making checks, but from what I can gather this doesn't always happen.

I obviously don't agree with animal activists who hurt people for their cause. I also think that the whole medical research industry is very corrupt.

Everyone is competing to find a cure for cancer or a cure for AIDS, so labs around the world are not sharing their research. They want to find the cures and they want to make money. As a result instead of 100 animals being used in a test, 1,000 will be used for the same experiment, but in different labs.

I think that animals are seen as amenities the same way as a piece of scientific equipment, not as sensitive beings whose lives should be valued. It's wrong that animals are just commodities for the medical research industry."

Three years ago, Sarah Roberts, 18, from Solihull, was diagnosed with cancer. Her treatment would not have been possible without the use of animal medical research

"When I first discovered I had cancer it was a complete shock. The doctor handled it well, but I cried on my mum's shoulder for about ten hours. I used to get really depressed but I realised I had to get on with my life and the people around me being so positive helped me do that.

First, I had my biopsy to check that the tumour was cancerous. Then I had an operation to remove the infected bone in my leg and fit a metal replacement.

I'm obviously biased when it comes to animal medical testing – I think it's fair enough. Activists will feel differently and that's their individual right, but they probably haven't needed painkillers and chemotherapy. I think animal research is a good thing, it's not as if there is a proper alternative yet.

If an animal activist had to choose between their life or that of a rat, the rat's probably going to die. It would be hard to be an activist if you'd been through a serious illness.

I feel strongly 'cause I've met so many people who've needed serious medical attention. Two of my friends have also been diagnosed this year. One with cancer, the other with leukaemia. When you experience such life-threatening illness you realise the importance of progress in medical research.

I'll have to have check-ups for another four years. I've just had one, but was given the all-clear for now. I'm feeling great at the moment.

I'm a living example that you can get through cancer and have a brilliant life. Since my illness, me and my family realise how precious human life actually is and if it takes an animal's life to preserve that, then so be it."

The two people interviewed on vivisection express very different views.

(?) *Make a chart like the one below. List the main points made by Judith and Sarah. The first two are done for you.*

Judith

Interested in animal rights since becoming a vegetarian.

Never allowed into labs to see how animals are treated during testing.

Sarah

Opinion influenced by her own experience of cancer.

There is currently no alternative to animal medical testing.

When presenting an argument, it is important to organise your ideas in a logical order and make your key points clearly. Now look at the following question.

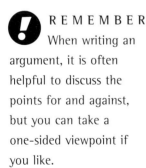

REMEMBER Plan your ideas first, and use phrases, such as the ones listed in 'Broadening your discussion' (below), to link ideas and introduce different points of view.

People who take part in dangerous sports, hobbies and expeditions risk their lives and sometimes the lives of the people who have to rescue them. Write about whether you think people should take part in dangerous activities like these.

(?) *List the key points you would include in answer to this question. It may help you to think about:*
- *examples of dangerous sports, hobbies or expeditions which people undertake*
- *reasons why people want to do these activities*
- *some of the problems that can arise*
- *whether there should be limits on what people are allowed to do.*

Broadening your discussion

REMEMBER When writing an argument, it is often helpful to discuss the points for and against, but you can take a one-sided viewpoint if you like.

The two people in the article on animal testing had very clear points of view on the subject. Their views were based on their personal experiences and opinions. Sometimes, however, you may not have a clear-cut point of view on a particular situation or topic. Maybe you have some sympathy with both sides of the argument. That's not a problem because you can use your ideas to develop a wider discussion on the given topic.

When discussing a range of different points of view, it is often helpful to link ideas by using words or phrases such as the following:

Alternatively . . . On the other hand . . . Some people believe that . . .
In contrast to this . . . Nevertheless . . . Similarly . . .
Perhaps the most important point is . . . This suggests that . . .

It is useful to have these words and phrases, and others like them, in your vocabulary. Then you will be ready to use them to broaden your discussion.

Reading fiction

📺 Looking at plot

The plot of a story or extract is the outline of the events that take place. However, the ways in which a writer tells the story to the reader are the most important thing.

Read the following story:

> I was walking down the street. I was with my friend Danny. We passed a shop. There were lots of shoppers. Suddenly a lady ran out of the shop. She shouted that her little boy had got lost. Many people ran around the shop looking for the little boy. Me and Danny joined in. We found the boy looking at toys. We took him back to his mother. She said thank you to us. So did the policeman. We went home and told our parents. They gave us money for the pictures and we went to see *Star Wars*.

This is the outline of quite an exciting story. The boys had become caught up in a real human drama. They played an active part and were rewarded. Yet the story comes across as very flat and dull. Why?

First of all, the author has not described the <u>setting</u> in a way that makes the reader really feel part of the story. There is no description of the noisy, crowded street or the bustling and busy store.

Secondly, the story is told in simple sentences. There is no <u>sentence variation</u> to move the story along or to build up tension.

Thirdly, there is no real attempt to use <u>expressive</u> words. The vocabulary is plain. The author has not used carefully chosen words that enable the reader to see and feel what is going on. The reader is told nothing of the feelings of the mother or boys in the search.

Finally, the author has not tried to <u>build up the story</u>. No thought has been given to building the exciting events into a climax, up to the point where the missing child is found.

Experienced authors know how to do these things well. They are features of writing that you will be expected to recognise in your reading.

Read this extract. It is the opening of a novel by Charles Dickens.

Passage 1: Great Expectations

Ours was the marsh country, down by the river within twenty miles of the sea. This bleak place overgrown with nettles was the churchyard. Philip Pirrip, my father, and Georgiana, my mother, were dead and buried here. The dark flat wilderness beyond the churchyard was the marshes. The low leaden line beyond was the river, and the small bundle of shivers growing afraid of it all and beginning to cry, was myself, Pip.

'Hold your noise!' cried a terrible voice, as a man started up from among the graves.

A fearful man, all in coarse grey, with a great iron on his leg. A man with no hat, and broken shoes, and with an old rag tied round his head. A man who had been soaked in water, and smothered in mud, and lamed by stones, and cut by flints, and stung by nettles, and torn by briars; who limped, and shivered, and glared, and growled; and whose teeth chattered in his head as he seized me by the chin.

'Tell us your name!' said the man. 'Quick!'

'Pip. Pip, sir.'

'Show us where you live,' said the man. 'Point out the place!'

I pointed to where our village lay, on the flat inshore among the alder-trees and pollards, a mile or more from the church.

The man, after looking at me for a moment, turned me upside down, and emptied my pockets. There was nothing in them but a piece of bread. He sat me on a high tombstone, trembling, while he ate the bread ravenously.

'Now then, lookee here!' said the man. 'Where's your mother?'

'There, sir!' said I.

He started, made a short run, and stopped and looked over his shoulder.

'There, sir!' I timidly exclaimed. 'Also Georgiana. That's my mother.'

'Oh!' said he, coming back. 'And is that your father along with your mother?'

'Yes, sir,' said I; 'him too, late of this parish.'

'Ha!' he muttered then, considering. 'Who d'ye live with – supposin' you're kindly let to live – which I han't made up my mind about?'

'My sister, sir – Mrs Joe Gargery – wife of Joe Gargery, the blacksmith, sir.'

'Blacksmith, eh?' said he. And looked down at his leg.

After darkly looking at his leg and at me several times, he came closer to my tombstone, took me by both arms, tilted me back as far as he could hold me, so that his eyes looked most powerfully down into mine, and mine looked most helplessly up into his.

'Now, lookee here,' he said, 'the question being whether you're to be let to live. You know what a file is?'

'Yes, sir.'

'And you know what wittles is?'

'Yes, sir.'

After each question he tilted me over a little more.

'You get me a file.' He tilted me again. 'And bring me, tomorrow morning early, that file and them wittles. You bring the lot to me, at that old Battery over yonder. You do it, and you never dare to say a word or dare to make a sign concerning your having seen such a person as me, and you shall live. You fail, and your heart and your liver shall be torn out, roasted and ate. Now, what do you say?'

I said that I would get him the file, and I would get him what broken bits of food I could, and I would come to him at the Battery, early in the morning.

'Now,' he pursued, 'you remember what you've undertook, and you remember that, young man, and you get home!'

'Goo–goodnight, sir,' I faltered.

He hugged his shuddering body in both his arms – and limped towards the low church wall. He got over it like a man whose legs were numbed and stiff, and then turned round to look for me. When I saw him turning, I set my face towards home, and made the best use of my legs.

REMEMBER
The author uses many devices to encourage you to continue reading the story. These include:
■ describing the setting
■ different sentence lengths, for variation
■ expressive words which bring scenes to life
■ building cleverly to a climax in order to keep you interested.

? *Now make a chart using the following four points as headings: Setting, Sentence variation, Expressive vocabulary and Build-up. Under each heading give examples of how Dickens displays these skills. The first one has been done for you.*

Setting	Sentence variation	Expressive vocabulary	Build-up
marsh country	uses both long and short sentences	'bleak' / 'dark flat'	tension builds as convict appears

The examiner will expect you to show your understanding of the skills the author uses to tell a story. It is not enough simply to describe the bare outline of the story. You must demonstrate that you recognise the devices that have contributed to an exciting piece of story-telling, and that have stopped it from being flat and boring.

Practice

How does Charles Dickens make the beginning of *Great Expectations* an exciting opening to a story?

📺🔊Looking at character

Creating believable characters who play a convincing part in a narrative is an essential part of good story-writing. What do the examiners expect of you when they ask you to write about character?

Think about the way you get to know the characters of real people in your life. You can see what they look like by observation. You could think of suitable words to describe their appearance. You can also learn about character from the things people say. Their words may give away their opinions on certain matters and tell you something about them, for example, whether they are kind / cruel / thoughtful / loyal / truthful / dishonest. You can also learn about character from the things other people say about them. You know whether or not you can trust these opinions.

(?) *Think of a person you know well. Make a chart with three columns. Give the columns the following headings: Appearance; What they say; What others say. Fill in the chart. From these ideas you can now write about the character of this person.*

❗ REMEMBER There are vital clues to look for in a character in fiction:
■ what does the character look like?
■ what does the character say?
■ what do the other characters in the book think of the character you are writing about?

Look again at the story on page 29 about the lost boy in the shop. One reason why it is dull is that the author has given no information about the character. He says nothing about himself or his friend, Danny, or about the mother of the lost boy. He says little about the policeman, only mentioning him briefly at the end. Think how much more interesting this story could have been if there was some information about these characters - information along the lines of the ideas you have just written down in the exercise above.

Now look back at the extract from *Great Expectations*. Notice how much information there is about the convict.

■ Look at the description of his appearance in the third paragraph.

■ Look at the words he speaks, particularly the threats he makes against Pip.

■ Look at Pip's reaction to the sight of the convict and to what the convict says.

This information builds up a picture of the convict. You can imagine his rough-looking condition and feel Pip's fear of him. These are the kinds of things you need to notice in your reading when you are looking at character.

Practice

Describe your reaction to the convict in the extract from *Great Expectations*.

In your answer you should write about:

■ the convict's appearance

■ what he says to Pip

■ the effect that the convict has on Pip.

◉Looking at language

REMEMBER
Words must be carefully chosen for effective writing. The author needs to describe settings and characters.

Authors choose their words very carefully. They may be describing a scene, or a character, or how a person is feeling. They want the reader to picture the scene, or react to the character, or recognise the feelings.

Look again at the story on page 29 of the boy lost in the shop. The author tells you nothing about the setting of the story – where it takes place or what the area looks like – nor do you learn about the feelings of the main characters. How did the lady feel when her child was returned to her? How did the boys feel as they took part in the search? What different feelings did they experience when they received their 'reward'? A good writer would have thought carefully about the words he was using, so that the readers could share the feelings of the main characters in the story.

Now look again at the extract from *Great Expectations* on page 30. Look at the words Dickens uses to set the scene in the first paragraph. What do you picture in your mind when you read the words 'dark flat wilderness' and 'low leaden line'? Think also about the words Dickens uses to describe Pip's feelings: 'the small bundle of shivers growing afraid of it all . . .'

REMEMBER
If the characters are speaking, the author needs to think about the style in which he or she writes their words. The author will probably want to make the style of a character's speech add to your ideas about the character.

Look at the words the convict uses: '"Now lookee here," he said, "the question being whether you're to be let to live . . ."' Imagine the effect of those words on Pip. Notice also that Dickens chooses to write the convict's speech in dialect, or local accent. This makes the story more realistic, but it also makes the convict seem rougher. How do you think a modern author, writing about a gangster threatening a frightened child, would write the gangster's speech?

(?) *Make a chart with two columns. Give one column the heading* Setting *and the other the heading* Convict's Speech. *Write down the different words Dickens uses for each of these topics. Why has he chosen these words? What effect does he want his words to have on the reader?*

Reading fiction

Practice

How does Dickens use carefully chosen language to add to the settings and characters in this extract from *Great Expectations* (page 30)? In your answer you should think about:

- the description of the setting at the start of the extract

- how Pip feels

- the character of the convict and his effect upon Pip

- the description of the convict at the end of the extract.

📺◉Reading poetry

In your Test, you may be asked to read and answer questions on a poem. Read this poem carefully several times.

Blackberry-Picking by Seamus Heaney

> Late August, given heavy rain and sun
> For a full week, the blackberries would ripen.
> At first, just one, a glossy purple clot
> Among others, red, green, hard as a knot.
> You ate that first one and its flesh was sweet
> Like thickened wine: summer's blood was in it
> Leaving stains upon the tongue and lust for
> Picking. Then red ones inked up and that hunger
> Sent us out with milk-cans, pea-tins, jam-pots
> Where briars scratched and wet grass bleached our boots.
> Round hayfields, cornfields and potato-drills
> We trekked and picked until the cans were full,
> Until the tinkling bottom had been covered
> With green ones, and on top big dark blobs burned
> Like a plate of eyes. Our hands were peppered
> With thorn pricks, our palms sticky as Bluebeard's.
>
> We hoarded the fresh berries in the byre.
> But when the bath was filled we found a fur,
> A rat-grey fungus, glutting on our cache.
> The juice was stinking too. Once off the bush
> The fruit fermented, the sweet flesh would turn sour.
> I always felt like crying. It wasn't fair
> That all the lovely canfuls smelt of rot.
> Each year I hoped they'd keep, knew they would not.

This section will look closely at Seamus Heaney's poem, *Blackberry-Picking*, to see how it has been written and what the poet wants to tell the reader in the poem. In many ways, the work you are doing here is similar to the work you did in the section on *Great Expectations*, except that this time you will be looking at verse rather than prose.

Look at what Heaney tells you about the events that occurred in the poem. He describes an incident at the end of the summer when he went with his friends to pick blackberries. Many of you will have had a similar experience, either in the wild or on Pick-Your-Own farms. But notice the way Heaney describes the incident; the detail he uses and the carefully chosen language. Heaney also describes his feelings: the excitement he experienced when the berries were picked compared to the disappointment he felt when he found that they would not keep fresh.

There are two key factors to bear in mind when reading poetry:

- the language the poet uses to describe incidents that are happening, or incidents he can remember

- the language the poet uses to describe feelings.

You can read more about these different types of language below.

Language for description

Look again at the first verse. Heaney wants to let the reader share in the memory and excitement of the picking. See how he uses colours: red, green, purple. These are the colours of the berry as it grows, but they are rich colours, too. Notice also how much he mentions the different senses:

- Touch: ' . . . hard as a knot . . . ' Here the poet uses a <u>simile</u>; this means he is saying that something is *like* something else. It's not only important to recognise the simile, you must also say why the poet has chosen it. In this case you might say that the knot makes you think of a knot in a rope, which is hard to the touch, or even a knot in a piece of wood, which is hard to cut through.

- Taste: ' . . . its flesh was sweet / Like thickened wine . . . ' This is another simile. Why do you think the poet has chosen to say that the berry's flesh was like thickened wine? He continues to describe the taste: 'summer's blood was in it . . . ' Here the poet uses a <u>metaphor</u>, where he actually describes one thing <u>as though it *were*</u> another thing. This imaginative writing brings to mind pictures of the berries growing in the summer and the colour and texture of the berry juice.

- Sight: ' . . . red ones inked up . . . ' This describes how the berries looked as they changed colour; ' . . . wet grass bleached our boots . . . ' describes the look of the boots the children were wearing. These images are both metaphors. Can you explain why they are imaginative ideas?

(?) *There are many individual words that describe the scene and the feelings of the children, for example: 'glossy purple clot'; 'lust'; 'trekked'; 'tinkling bottom'; 'Like a plate of eyes'; 'peppered'. Copy these words down on one side of a page. On the other side, try to explain why you think the poet has chosen to use them.*

! **R E M E M B E R** You need to explain what effect a simile has and why it is successful.

Reading fiction

KS3 BITESIZEenglish 35

Language for feelings

In the first verse, Heaney uses words to describe the excitement of the children. You have already looked at some examples of these. In the second verse, he explores different feelings; they <u>contrast</u> strongly with the feelings in the first verse.

! REMEMBER
When a poet says that a thing is <u>like</u> something else, this is a simile.

Notice the powerful words used to describe the children's attempts to keep the berries fresh:

- 'hoarded', a word often used to describe misers hiding their money,

- 'rat-grey', to describe the colour. This is not just a contrast with the rich colours of the first verse; many people find rats really unpleasant creatures.

! REMEMBER
When a poet says that a thing <u>is</u> something else, this is a metaphor.

Powerful words are used to describe the smell and texture of the gathered berries: 'glutting', 'stinking' and 'sour'. All these words reflect how desperate the writer was to keep the berries. Alongside the description of excited `feelings in the first verse, they help to convey the feeling of how bitterly disappointed the young Seamus must have been when 'he felt like crying' and when 'the lovely canfuls smelt of rot.'

Practice

How does Seamus Heaney enable the reader to share his memories of picking blackberries as a young boy? In your answer you should write about:

- the scene Heaney sets at the start

- the details he uses to help you to see the whole picture

- how his feelings change between the beginning and the end of the poem

- examples of Heaney's imaginative use of words which help you to share his memories.

Ⓣ⒱Reading between the lines

Developing comment and personal response

Sometimes you need to think carefully about exactly what the poet is saying. Is he simply asking you to share a memory or some feelings, or is he trying to get you to think about something else as well, which affects us all?

Look again at *Blackberry-Picking*.

The forcefulness of the language and the attention to detail tell you that this is a clear and powerful memory for the poet. For example, the use of the word 'lust' suggests an extremely powerful desire. There are links with flesh and blood in the first verse: 'clot', 'flesh was sweet', 'thickened wine' and 'summer's blood', all refer to things which are vital for life.

The power of the words suggests that Heaney is not simply remembering an incident from his childhood. He is using his memory to persuade the reader to share his thoughts about something more important. What might that be?

Remember the circumstances of the incident. The poet and his friends had gone out to pick berries. They had taken the fruits from the natural world, tried to keep them fresh and had watched them rot and grow sour. Could the poet be making a point about interfering with the environment unnecessarily? Or is he saying that, sometimes in life, the beautiful things we try to keep may lose their attraction and be a disappointment to us?

As with many poems, there are a range of possible comments you could make. Your personal response is as valuable as anyone else's. But you must be able to <u>support your ideas</u> with quotations from the poem. There is a huge difference between sensible, supported comments and wild guesses which have no support from the poem.

Practice

In the poem *Blackberry-Picking*, Seamus Heaney describes his memory of an incident that is important to him. Why is this incident important to him? How does Heaney use language to persuade you that the incident is important to him? In your answer you should write about:

- the particular words and details he uses in his description of the incident

- the particular words and details he uses when describing his feelings

- your own personal response to the poem, with appropriate quotations.

Imaginative writing

📺 🎧 Narrative/personal writing

In previous papers the writing questions have included at least one task that asks students to write about a real or imaginary event or experience. Here is an example:

Write about an incident in which you had to leave a place you knew well. You could write about a real or an imaginary experience.

If you choose to write about a real event, then you are drawing on your own experience and using something that has actually happened. This is called personal writing. If you decide to make something up then you are writing fiction. Either way, you are going to be writing a narrative. Good narratives have certain characteristics:

■ **an interesting subject**

Whether you are writing from personal or imagined experience, you need to choose the subject of your narrative carefully, so that it will be of interest to your reader. Some students make the mistake of trying to do too much. You only have about forty minutes to plan, write and check your work. There is no point trying to cover a life-story in that time. Better to focus on one day in a life-time, or even one hour.

■ **a clearly-defined structure**

You only have a short time in which to plan and write your narrative. You need to structure your ideas very carefully, so that the sequence of events is clear to your reader. It is not necessary to tell your readers everything that has happened before the main part of the narrative starts, nor to tell them everything that happens at the end. It is possible to leave them wondering what will happen next, to create an air of mystery.

■ **convincing characters**

It is best to focus on one or two characters and to try and make them 'come alive'. Avoid including too many characters; lists of names fill space, but they will confuse your reader and they are not very interesting.

■ **a sense of setting**

Give your reader a clear sense of setting. It may be in a large place, like a city, or a very small one, such as a room. Aim to describe it in enough detail so that the reader can imagine it.

❗ REMEMBER Describe a few characters, in a clear setting, over a short time period, for a successful narrative.

■ **variety of sentence structures and vocabulary**

Aim to use a range of simple, compound and complex sentence structures. Choose your words carefully so that you demonstrate a range of vocabulary to your examiner.

Read the following short story.

❗ REMEMBER
Variety of sentence structure and vocabulary is an important aspect of all your writing.

Passage 1: I Used to Live Here Once by Jean Rhys

She was standing by the river looking at the stepping stones and remembering each one. There was the round unsteady stone, the pointed one, the flat one in the middle – the safe stone where you could stand and look around. The next wasn't so safe for when the river was full the water flowed over it and even when it showed dry it was slippery. But after that it was easy and soon she was standing on the other side.

The road was much wider than it used to be but the work had been done carelessly. The felled trees had not been cleared away and the bushes looked trampled. Yet it was the same road and she walked along feeling extraordinarily happy.

It was a fine day, a blue day. The only thing was that the sky had a glassy look she didn't remember. That was the only word she could think of. Glassy. She turned the corner, saw that what had been the old pavement had been taken up, and there too the road was much wider, but it had the same unfinished look.

She came to the worn stones that led up to the house and her heart began to beat. The screw pine was gone, so was the mock summer house called the ajoupa, but the clove tree was still there and at the top of the steps the rough lawn stretched away, just as she had remembered it. She stopped and looked toward the house that had been added to and painted white. It was strange to see a car standing in front of it.

There were two children under the big mango tree, a boy and a little girl, and she waved to them and called 'Hello' but they didn't answer her or turn their heads. Very fair children, as Europeans born in the West Indies so often are: as if the white blood is asserting itself against all odds.

The grass was yellow in the hot sunlight as she walked towards them. When she was quite close she called again, shyly: 'Hello'. Then, 'I used to live here once,' she said.

Still they didn't answer. When she said for the third time

'Hello' she was quite near them. Her arms went out instinctively with the longing to touch them.

It was the boy who turned, his grey eyes looked straight into hers. His expression didn't change. He said, 'Hasn't it gone cold all of a sudden. D'you notice? Let's go in.' 'Yes let's,' said the girl.

Her arms fell to her side as she watched them running across the grass to the house. That was the first time she knew.

Think about:

subject: what is the story about?

structure: how are the ideas organised? Think about where the woman is when the story starts and where she is at the end. How do her impressions develop and alter? How does the writer create a sense of mystery in the last sentence of the story?

setting: what do you learn about the setting? How do you know that the woman is familiar with the place?

character: who is the main character in the story? What do you learn about her background and what she is like?

sentence structures and vocabulary: find examples of simple, compound and complex sentences. How are the words used to suggest a sense of familiarity in the first paragraph? What use is made of colour in the passage as a whole?

Now that you have examined this short story in detail, try writing your own.

(?) *Write about someone who has an experience of being isolated and cut-off from other people. You could write about yourself or someone else. You could base your writing on a real or an imaginary experience.*

Narrative voice

The story on page 39 is written in the third person. The author is standing back and writing about someone else, in other words the woman, or 'she'.

Some stories are written in the first person narrative. In these, the author tells about himself or herself, in other words 'I', or 'me'. This creates a greater sense of being personally involved in the story. Stories can also be written in the second person – 'you' – though this form is used less frequently.

Tension and suspense

Questions in the Test may occasionally ask you to build up a feeling of tension or suspense in your writing. Here is an example:

(?) *Write about someone who is frightened or nervous but who tries to overcome these feelings.*
In your writing you could:
- *write about a real or imaginary event*
- *try to build up a feeling of tension or suspense.*

Read the following passage from *The Lonely One* by Ray Bradbury. Look at how Bradbury uses sentence length, images and paragraphing to create an effect of fear and tension.

Passage 2: The Lonely One by Ray Bradbury

She ran across the bridge.

Oh God, God, please, please let me get up the hill! Now up the path, now between the hills, oh God, it's dark, and everything so far away. If I screamed now it wouldn't help; I can't scream anyway. Here's the top of the path, here's the street, oh, God, please let me be safe, if I get home safe I'll never go out alone; I was a fool, let me admit it, I was a fool. I didn't know what terror was, but if you let me get home from this I'll never go without Helen or Francine again! Here's the street. Across the street!

She crossed the street and rushed up the sidewalk.

Oh God, the porch! My house! Oh God, please give me time to get inside and lock the door and I'll be safe!

And there, silly thing to notice – why did she notice, instantly, no time, no time – but there it was anyway, flashing by – there on the porch rail, the half-filled glass of lemonade she had abandoned a long time, a year, half an evening ago! The lemonade glass sitting calmly, imperturbably there on the rail . . . and . . .

She heard her clumsy feet on the porch and listened and felt her hands scrabbling and ripping at the lock with the key. She heard her heart. She heard her inner voice screaming.

The key fit.

Unlock the door, quick, quick!

The door opened.

! REMEMBER
Look at the punctuation and at who is narrating the story, too.

Imaginative writing

Now, inside. Slam it!

She slammed the door.

'Now lock it, bar it, lock it!' she gasped wretchedly.

'Lock it, tight, tight!'

The door was locked and bolted tight.

The music stopped. She listened to her heart again and the sound of it diminishing into silence.

Home! Oh God, safe at home! Safe, safe and safe at home! She slumped against the door. Safe, safe. Listen. Not a sound. Safe, safe, oh thank God, safe at home. I'll never go out at night again ever. Safe, oh safe, safe home, so good, so good, safe! Safe inside, the door locked. Wait.

Look out the window.

She looked.

Why, there's no one there at all! Nobody! There was nobody following me at all. Nobody running after me. She got her breath and almost laughed at herself.

Bradbury builds up tension in this story using a number of different techniques.

(?) *Find examples of each of the following:*
- *variety in sentence length with extensive use of short sentences*
- *range of punctuation including exclamation marks (!), hyphens (-) and ellipsis (. . .)*
- *a series of very short paragraphs*
- *free movement between the third person narrative and the first person narrative.*

Look at the examples you have selected. What effects do they create? Try to use these effects in your own writing.

Practice

Now that you have examined this short story in detail, try writing your own. Aim to use the techniques Bradbury uses to create a feeling of tension.

Write about a frightening encounter with an animal.

In your writing you could:

- write about a real or imaginary event

- try to build up a feeling of tension or suspense.

⊞⊚Descriptive writing

In your test you may be asked to describe a person or a place or an experience. Your aim is to make whatever, or whoever, it is you are describing seem real to the reader. There are four main areas you need to consider when thinking about descriptive writing:

- range of detail
- use of descriptive language
- atmosphere and mood
- organisation.

Range of detail

If your reader is to get a clear picture of what you are describing then you need to give plenty of detail in your description. In a way you are painting a picture with words and your reader needs to be able to see what is in your mind.

In the following extract, Roald Dahl describes the man who has come to deal with a snake that has been found in the living-room. As you are reading, note the amount of detail Dahl gives in his description.

Passage 1: The Green Mamba by Roald Dahl

The snake-man was small and very old, probably over seventy. He wore leather boots made of thick cowhide and he had long gauntlet-type gloves on his hands made of the same stuff. The gloves reached above his elbows. In his right hand he carried an extraordinary implement, an eight-foot-long wooden pole with a forked end. The two prongs of the fork were made, so it seemed, of black rubber, about an inch thick and quite flexible, and it was clear that if the fork was pressed against the ground the two prongs would bend outwards, allowing the neck of the fork to go down as close to the ground as necessary. In his left hand he carried an ordinary brown sack.

Donald Macfarlane, the snake-man, may have been old and small but he was an impressive-looking character. His eyes were pale blue, deep-set in a face round and dark and wrinkled as a walnut. Above the blue eyes, the eyebrows were thick and startlingly white but the hair on his head was almost black. In spite of the thick leather boots, he moved like a leopard, with soft slow cat-like strides.

! REMEMBER
Look at how Dahl describes how the man looks and moves, his clothes and his tools.

Imaginative writing

(?) *1 List the different details you are given about the snake-man. The first three are: small / very old / wore leather boots.*

2 Think of a person you know well. List the different details you could use to describe this person.

3 Notice the development of detail used to describe the fork that the snake-man carries: 'In his right hand he carried an extraordinary implement, an eight-foot-long wooden pole with a forked end. The two prongs of the fork were made, so it seemed, of black rubber, about an inch thick and quite flexible, and it was clear that if the fork was pressed against the ground the two prongs would bend outwards, allowing the neck of the fork to go down as close to the ground as necessary.' Dahl describes the fork in great detail because it plays an important part later on in the capture of the snake.

Choose one item from the list you made in question 2. Write two or three sentences in which you develop the description of this one item.

4 Notice the way in which Dahl describes the movements of the snake-man: 'he moved like a leopard, with slow cat-like strides'. What words would you use to describe the movements of the person you are thinking of? Can you think of a simile that would help you to describe them effectively?

5 Now that you have thought carefully about the person, write a detailed description of him or her.

Use of descriptive language

There are many ways of using language to create an effective description. Take a simple sentence: The trees moved in the breeze.

You could make this more descriptive in the following ways:

- by adding adjectives: The <u>tall</u>, <u>willowy</u> trees moved in the <u>soft</u> breeze.

- by changing the verb and adding an adverb: The trees <u>swayed gently</u> in the breeze.

- by using a simile to help describe the trees: The trees moved in the breeze like <u>sails over the water</u>.

If you put them all together you now have this sentence: The tall, willowy trees swayed gently in the soft breeze like sails over the water.

(?) *Try to do the same with each of these simple sentences:*
The sun shone in the sky.
The flower grew in the garden.

Introducing adjectives, adverbs and similes can improve the effectiveness of your writing, but they must be appropriate. It is important not to overdo it.

(!) REMEMBER
Your aim is to write a description that helps your reader see what is in your mind.

Read the following extract carefully. In it Sky sees the rubbish tip, her new home, for the first time:

Passage 2: Throwaways by Ian Strachan

They soon found themselves moving between row after row of primitive shelters. Some, so far as Sky could see, were made from nothing more substantial than cardboard boxes. Most leaned heavily on their neighbours for support giving the impression that if one should collapse, all the others would go down like a run of dominoes.

One had a piece of old carpet slung over it for extra protection from the weather. Another consisted solely of a single sheet of rusty, corrugated iron, bent over to form a long, low tunnel. There were also several tents, patchwork quilts of rags and plastic bags, thrown over flimsy frames.

Many of the homes were lit with candles, or oil lamps, by whose pale, flickering light Sky made out shadowy figures moving around inside.

To Sky the place seemed like a cross between an ant hill and a rabbit warren. Over it all hung the hot, sour smell of the Tip and the sound of stray dogs, barking as they fought over scraps of food . . .

As they passed through row after row of huts, Sky had the uncomfortable feeling of being watched with suspicion, if not hostility, by hundreds of pairs of unseen eyes.

REMEMBER
Look at how adjectives, adverbs and similes help to create an effective description.

(?) *1 In the first paragraph, the author gives details of what the shelters look like. Read it again carefully. Can you imagine them?*

2 What is the effect of the verbs 'slung' in line 7 and 'hung' in line 16?

3 Underline the adjectives used in the passage. Which ones do you think are particularly effective? Try to explain why.

4 What similes does the writer use to describe: a) the shelters, b) the place? What do these add to the description?

Atmosphere and mood

In the extract above you read about a place that has a hint of danger. The author suggests this by telling you about the 'shadowy figures, the sour smell, the sound of stray dogs' and the 'hundreds of pairs of unseen eyes'. The author is creating a sense of atmosphere and mood. He doesn't just describe

Imaginative writing

what can be seen, but touches on the smell and the sound of the place and the things that can be felt but not clearly defined. By doing so he creates a sense of unease and danger; this is a place where something unpleasant is likely to happen.

In the following extract from the opening of *Bleak House*, the author Charles Dickens describes the fog that surrounds the High Court of Chancery, the central London law court.

Passage 3: Bleak House

REMEMBER
Think carefully about the kind of atmosphere and mood the author is trying to conjure up.

Fog everywhere. Fog up the river, where it flows among green aits and meadows; fog down the river, where it rolls defiled among the tiers of shipping, and the waterside pollutions of a great (and dirty) city. Fog on the Essex marshes, fog on the Kentish heights. Fog creeping into the cabooses of collier-brigs, fog lying out on the yards, and hovering in the rigging of great ships; fog drooping on the gunwales of barges and small boats. Fog in the eyes and throats of ancient Greenwich pensioners, wheezing by the firesides of their wards; fog in the stem and bowl of the afternoon pipe of the wrathful skipper, down in his close cabin; fog cruelly pinching the toes and fingers of his shivering little 'prentice boy on deck. Chance people on the bridges peeping over the parapets into a nether sky of fog, with fog all round them, as if they were up in a balloon, and hanging in the misty clouds.

Gas looming through the fog in divers places in the streets, much as the sun may, from the spongy fields, be seen to loom by husbandman and ploughboy. Most of the shops lighted two hours before their time – as the gas seems to know, for it has a haggard and unwilling look.

The raw afternoon is rawest, and the dense fog is densest, and the muddy streets are muddiest, near that leaden-headed old obstruction, appropriate ornament for the threshold of a leaden-headed old corporation: Temple Bar. And hard by Temple Bar, in Lincoln's Inn Hall, at the very heart of the fog, sits the Lord High Chancellor in his High Court of Chancery.

In this description, Dickens starts with the simple statement: 'Fog everywhere.' Look how he then explores in detail the impact of the fog on the environment.

? *1 The fog is made to seem almost human. Find as many examples as you can of the way in which Dickens describes its movements and actions.*

2 Dickens shows us that the fog is everywhere. What places and people are affected by it?

3 Think about fog and what it is like. What kind of atmosphere and mood does Dickens build up in this description of it?

4 Why does Dickens carefully build up this description of the fog? What is he trying to emphasise? The clue to the answer is in the last line of the passage.

Organisation

In the extract from *Bleak House* you saw how Dickens started with the simple statement 'Fog everywhere', and then went on to describe the fog and its effects. He steadily built up the detail to give emphasis to the fact that at the very heart of all this fog sat the Lord High Chancellor. The ideas were organised deliberately to produce this effect.

Organisation is an important part of your descriptive writing. Work your way through stages 1–5 to help you complete the following task:

? *Write an article for a travel magazine, describing a place that is beautiful and mysterious.*

1 Choose a suitable place. Picture it in your mind. Make a list of details about its appearance and what makes it beautiful. Think of interesting adjectives that you could use to describe each of these details.

2 Think about what the place feels like. What makes it mysterious? It might help to think of it at different times of day. At what time of day is it most mysterious? Why is this? What words and phrases could you use to describe its mysterious atmosphere and mood?

3 Decide whether you are going to write your description in the first, second or third person. Where, as the writer, are you going to be? Will you be: a) looking in at it from the outside, b) wandering around in it, c) somewhere else, thinking about the place?

4 Decide on the sequence of things you are going to write about and make a paragraph plan.

5 Think of a good way of starting your description. Here are some possibilities:

■ *In the twilight of a cool, autumn day the lakeside forest is transformed into an eerie and mysterious world.*

■ *I look ahead of me and gaze in wonder.*

■ *The sun shines relentlessly on the beautiful city of . . .*

6 Once you have finished your description, read it carefully. Does it paint a picture of the place that was in your mind? Are there any details or words you could add that would make your description more effective?

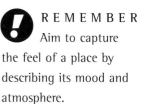 **REMEMBER** Aim to capture the feel of a place by describing its mood and atmosphere.

Imaginative writing

Shakespeare

As part of your KS3 National Test you will be expected to comment on a key scene from a play by William Shakespeare. You will have prepared the play in class. In the test you will have a choice of two key scenes. You must choose one scene and answer a question on it.

What will the examiners look for?

In your answer the examiners will be looking for, and awarding marks for, your ability to write about the following:

- the behaviour of the characters in the key scene; you may also link the characters' actions here to their actions in other parts of the play, especially if they are either very similar or very different.

- the reasons why the characters behave the way they do. Here again, there may be interesting links with other parts of the play.

- the way in which the story is developing. Is this a moment of great suspense in the story?

- whether the writer prepares the reader for what happens next.

- the language that Shakespeare uses. How does he make the actions and feelings of the characters come alive?

- the effect the scene has on the people watching the play. Is the audience frightened, amused, horrified, puzzled?

- the way in which the scene might be presented on stage. What sets might the director use? Would the director ask the actors to speak their lines in a certain way? If so, describe the different ways in which the actors would perform their lines. Where on the stage might the director want the actors to stand?

How do you answer questions like these?

This might all sound a bit scary at first glance. However, as you work through the revision process and focus on the key scene you are studying, your task will become less confusing.

You are not expected to come up with all these ideas to answer a single question. Different types of question will ask for different types of answer. You can choose the type of question you think you can answer best.

How to approach a chosen scene

Start by looking at a short piece of writing by Shakespeare, the opening scene of his play *Macbeth*. Concentrate on the language used and the drama of the action – the way in which it prepares the audience for events to come.

Passage 1: Macbeth

Act 1, Scene 1. *An open place. Thunder and lightning.*

Enter three Witches.

1 Witch:	When shall we three meet again?	
	In thunder, lightning, or in rain?	
2 Witch:	When the hurlyburly's done,	
	When the battle's lost and won:	
3 Witch:	That will be 'ere the set of sun.	5
1 Witch:	Where's the place?	
2 Witch:	Upon the heath:	
3 Witch:	There to meet with Macbeth.	
1 Witch:	I come, Graymalkin!	
2 Witch:	Paddock calls.	
3 Witch:	Anon!	
All:	Fair is foul, and foul is fair:	12
	Hover through the fog and filthy air.	

Witches vanish.

> **REMEMBER**
> This is a play to be seen in a theatre. Always keep in mind what it would have looked like to a seventeenth-century audience, seeing it for the very first time.

Effect on the audience

The first idea to consider in this scene is the effect it would have had on Shakespeare's audience. Shakespeare lived from 1564 until 1623. *Macbeth* was written in 1606. In Shakespeare's time people did not find witches humorous as we do today. Witches were still being burned at the stake.

There was widespread belief in witches and their evil powers. Their appearance at the start of the play would have filled the audience with uncertainty and horror. The witches refer to Graymalkin (a grey cat) and Paddock (a toad). This would have made them more believable as these animals were often linked with witches, as their 'familiars'.

REMEMBER
Try to pick out single words and groups of words, and think about why the writer has decided to use those particular words.

The language of the scene

Look at how the language of the scene adds to the atmosphere. Notice how the witches speak in verse. Perhaps a director could suggest that the actors make these words sound like evil chants? Notice how the words suggest confusion and opposition: 'hurlyburly', 'battle's lost', 'fair is foul, and foul is fair'. The words create an atmosphere of fighting and struggle which persists for the rest of the play. Also, the third witch calls Macbeth by name. This adds to the mystery. What do these evil creatures want with Macbeth? Is he one of them?

Shakespeare's presentation of ideas

The next point to look at is the way the setting works alongside the words to build up atmosphere. Theatre in Shakespeare's time had no dramatic special effects like film studios do today. The only special effects Shakespeare had at his disposal were descriptive words. So the witches talk about thunder, lightning and rain, fog and filthy air. How might the director emphasise these extreme weather conditions? To Shakespeare's audience, dramatic weather meant dramatic events for humankind. Normally, these events brought chaos and confusion. *Macbeth* was written one year after the Gunpowder Plot and the execution of Guy Fawkes. So the mention of plots and trouble in the country in *Macbeth* would have had an immediate impact on Shakespeare's audience.

What have you learnt?

In this short scene we have managed to touch upon many of the things the examiners are looking for:

- the presentation of ideas

- the behaviour of the characters

- the introduction of a storyline

- language in use

- the effect on the audience

- possible presentations on the stage.

REMEMBER
It is not enough just to know what happens in the scene. You must write about characters and their relationships with each other.

In the longer key scenes there is plenty of material from which to construct an effective examination answer. You can show your understanding of all the aspects of the scene and give the answers the examiners are looking for.

Practice

How does Shakespeare use the witches, and what they say, to create a dramatic opening to *Macbeth*?

Think about how you would direct a group of actors to perform this scene, and what stage set you would use.

🖵🔊Characters' thoughts

One type of question on the Shakespeare paper will ask you to follow the thoughts and feelings of one of the main characters in a key scene.

This section looks at another extract from *Macbeth*. In the following scene, Macbeth has second thoughts about the plan to kill the king, Duncan, and Lady Macbeth tries to persuade him to go ahead with it.

Passage 1: Macbeth

Act 1, Scene 7. *A Room in the castle.*

Hautboys and torches. Enter a Sewer, and divers Servants with dishes and service over the stage. Then enter Macbeth.

Macbeth: If it were done when 'tis done, then 'twere well
It were done quickly. If the assassination
Could trammel up the consequence, and catch,
With his surcease, success; that but this blow
Might be the be-all and the end-all, here,   5
But here, upon this bank and shoal of time,
We'd jump the life to come. But in these cases,
We still have judgment here, that we but teach
Bloody instructions, which, being taught, return
To plague the inventor. This even-handed justice   10
Commends the ingredience of our poison'd chalice
To our own lips. He's here in double trust:
First, as I am his kinsman and his subject,
Strong both against the deed; then, as his host,
Who should against his murderer shut the door,   15
Not bear the knife myself. Besides, this Duncan
Hath borne his faculties so meek, hath been
So clear in his great office, that his virtues
Will plead like angels, trumpet-tongued, against
The deep damnation of his taking-off;   20
And pity, like a naked new-born babe,
Striding the blast, or heaven's cherubim, hors'd
Upon the sightless couriers of the air,
Shall blow the horrid deed in every eye,
That tears shall drown the wind. I have no spur   25
To prick the sides of my intent, but only
Vaulting ambition, which o'erleaps itself,
And falls on the other. *Enter Lady Macbeth.*
How now, what news?

Lady Macbeth: He has almost supp'd. Why have you left   30
the chamber?

Macbeth: Hath he ask'd for me?

Lady Macbeth: Know you not he has?

Macbeth: We will proceed no further in this business.
            He hath honour'd me of late; and I have bought
            Golden opinions from all sorts of people,
            Which would be worn now in their newest gloss,
            Not cast aside so soon.

Lady Macbeth: Was the hope drunk
            Wherein you dress'd yourself? hath it slept since?   39
            And wakes it now to look so green and pale
            At what it did so freely? From this time
            Such I account thy love. Art thou afeard
            To be the same in thine own act and valour
            As thou art in desire? Wouldst thou have that   44
            Which thou esteem'st the ornament of life,
            And live a coward in thine own esteem,
            Letting 'I dare not' wait upon 'I would',
            Like the poor cat i' the adage?

Macbeth: Prithee, peace;   49
            I dare do all that may become a man;
            Who dares do more is none.

Lady Macbeth: What beast was't then
            That made you break this enterprise to me?
            When you durst do it, then you were a man;
            And to be more than what you were, you would   55
            Be so much more the man. Nor time, nor place,
            Did then adhere, and yet you would make both;
            They have made themselves, and that their fitness now
            Does unmake you. I have given suck, and know
            How tender 'tis to love the babe that milks me: 60
            I would, while it was smiling in my face,
            Have pluck'd my nipple from his boneless gums,
            And dash'd the brains out, had I so sworn
            As you have done to this.

Macbeth: If we should fail?

Lady Macbeth: We fail!
            But screw your courage to the sticking place,   67
            And we'll not fail. When Duncan is asleep,
            (Whereto the rather shall his day's hard journey
            Soundly invite him) his two chamberlains
            Will I with wine and wassail so convince
            That memory, the warder of the brain,   72
            Shall be a fume, and the receipt of reason
            A limbec only: When in swinish sleep
            Their drenched natures lie as in a death,
            What cannot you and I perform upon

	The unguarded Duncan? what not put upon	77
	His spongy officers; who shall bear the guilt	
	Of our great quell?	
Macbeth:	Bring forth men-children only,	
	For thy undaunted mettle should compose	
	Nothing but males. Will it not be receiv'd,	
	When we have mark'd with blood those sleepy two	83
	Of his own chamber, and us'd their very daggers,	
	That they have done't?	
Lady Macbeth:	Who dares receive it other,	
	As we shall make our griefs and clamour roar	
	Upon his death?	
Macbeth:	I am settled, and bend up	
	Each corporal agent to this terrible feat.	90
	Away, and mock the time with fairest show:	
	False face must hide what the false heart doth know.	
Exeunt.		

What do you think Lady Macbeth's thoughts and feelings are at this point in the play? Look at her conversation with Macbeth. Remember what has just happened. The audience has heard Macbeth's <u>soliloquy</u>, in which he expresses doubt about the wisdom of their plan, fears its consequences and reveals his respect for Duncan. He knows that he is about to commit a really evil deed. How do you think Lady Macbeth would feel upon finding him in this state? Her feelings are revealed in the discussion that follows.

(?) *Write down a summary of Macbeth's concerns and a separate summary of Lady Macbeth's responses. For example, in lines 33-37, Macbeth expresses concern about ruining his reputation; in lines 38-48, Lady Macbeth is scornful about her husband's change of mind and accuses him of cowardice. In each case, write down suitable direct quotations from the play.*

Use this to develop your reading of Lady Macbeth's thoughts and feelings.

■ Lady Macbeth is scornful of Macbeth's cowardice, determined to change his mind and confident in her ability to do so, even though his arguments are carefully thought out and well-presented.

■ As she deals with Macbeth's uncertainty, think about the way in which her thoughts would affect her feelings towards her husband and her ambitions to gain the throne of Scotland.

There are also opportunities to connect your ideas with the rest of the play:

■ Why does Macbeth respect Duncan?

■ How did Macbeth acquire the reputation that is so important to him?

■ Is Macbeth's fear that violence will bring about more violence borne out by the rest of the play?

REMEMBER
To understand characters' thoughts and feelings you need to look closely at what they say. You also need to look closely at how they react to what others are saying and doing around them.

REMEMBER
A soliloquy is a solo speech in which a character often reveals what he or she is thinking and feeling.

REMEMBER
Take the opportunity to link ideas expressed in the key scene with other events in the play.

Writing in role

One of the questions on your key scenes will ask you to assume the role of a character and to write out their response to the events in that scene.

This section looks at an extract from *Twelfth Night*, Act II, Scene 5. You will be asked to use the character of Malvolio to practise your role-writing response.

! **R E M E M B E R**
You will need to support your ideas with well-chosen and appropriate references and quotations.

Remind yourself what you have learnt about Malvolio up to this point in the play. Malvolio is the steward in the great house of Olivia. He is an important person with rank in the household – but he is a servant. Sir Toby Belch and Sir Andrew Aguecheek do not observe the serious tone of the rest of the house following the death of Olivia's brother. But, like Olivia, Sir Toby and Andrew are aristocrats, and Malvolio has no control over them. He has some control over other servants like Maria, Feste and Fabian, but they often outwit him.

Passage 1: Twelfth Night

Act II, Scene 5.

Olivia's garden.

Enter Sir Toby Belch, Sir Andrew Aguecheek, and Fabian.

Sir Toby: Come thy ways, Signior Fabian.

Fabian: Nay, I'll come; if I lose a scruple of this sport, let me be boiled to death with melancholy.

Sir Toby: Wouldst thou not be glad to have the niggardly rascally sheep-biter come by some notable shame?   5

Fabian: I would exult, man: you know, he brought me out o' favour with my lady about a bear-baiting here.

Sir Toby: To anger him, we'll have the bear again; and we will fool him black and blue:—shall we not, Sir Andrew?

Sir Andrew: An we do not, it is pity of our lives.   10

Enter Maria.

Sir Toby: Here comes the little villain:—How now, my metal of India?

Maria: Get ye all three into the box-tree. Malvolio's coming down this walk. He has been yonder i' the sun, practising behaviour to his own shadow this half-hour. Observe him, for the love of mockery, for I know this letter will make a contemplative idiot of him. Close, in the name of jesting! *[The men hide themselves.]* Lie thou there; *[throws down a letter]* for here comes the trout that must be caught with tickling.   20

Exit Maria. Enter Malvolio.

Malvolio: 'Tis but fortune; all is fortune. Maria once told me she did affect me, and I have heard herself

come thus near, that, should she fancy, it should
be one of my complexion. Besides, she uses me
with a more exalted respect than any one else
that follows her. What should I think on 't?   26

Sir Toby: Here's an overweening rogue!

Fabian: O, peace! Contemplation makes a rare turkey-
cock of him! how he jets under his advanced plumes!

Sir Andrew: 'Slight, I could so beat the rogue:–   30

Sir Toby: Peace, I say.

Malvolio: To be Count Malvolio;–

Sir Toby: Ah, rogue!

Sir Andrew: Pistol him, pistol him.

Sir Toby: Peace, peace!   35

Malvolio: There is example for 't; the Lady of the Strachy
married the yeoman of the wardrobe.

Sir Andrew: Fie on him, Jezebel!

Fabian: O, peace! Now he's deeply in; look, how
imagination blows him.   40

Malvolio: Having been three months married to her, sitting
in my state–

Sir Toby: O, for a stone-bow to hit him in the eye!

Malvolio: Calling my officers about me, in my branched
velvet gown, having come from a day-bed,
where I have left Olivia sleeping: 45

Sir Toby: Fire and brimstone!

Fabian: O, peace, peace!

Malvolio: And then to have the humour of state, and after
a demure travel of regard,–telling them I know
my place, as I would they should do theirs,–to
ask for my kinsman Toby:

Sir Toby: Bolts and shackles!   52

Fabian: O, peace, peace, peace! Now, now.

Malvolio: Seven of my people, with an obedient start, make
out for him. I frown the while, and, perchance,
wind up my watch, or play with my some rich
jewel. Toby approaches; curtsies there to me:

Sir Toby: Shall this fellow live?

Fabian: Though our silence be drawn from us with cars,
yet peace.   59

Malvolio: I extend my hand to him thus, quenching my
familiar smile with an austere regard of control:

Sir Toby: And does not Toby take you a blow o' the lips
then?   62

Malvolio: Saying, "Cousin Toby, my fortunes having cast me on your niece, give me this prerogative of speech:"–

Sir Toby: What, what?

Malvolio: "You must amend your drunkenness."

Sir Toby: Out, scab!   67

Fabian: Nay, patience, or we break the sinews of our plot.

Malvolio: "Besides, you waste the treasure of your time
with a foolish knight;"

Sir Andrew: That's me, I warrant you.

Malvolio: "One Sir Andrew:"

Sir Andrew: I knew 'twas I; for many do call me fool.   72

Malvolio: What employment have we here? *[Taking up the letter.]*

Fabian: Now is the woodcock near the gin.

Sir Toby: O peace! and the spirit of humours intimate
reading aloud to him!

Malvolio: By my life, this is my lady's hand: these be her
very C's, her U's, and her T's; and thus makes she
her great P's. It is, in contempt of question, her hand.   78

Sir Andrew: Her C's, her U's, and her T's. Why that?

Malvolio [reads]: "To the unknown beloved, this, and my
good wishes." Her very phrases!–By your leave,
wax.–Soft!–And the impressure her Lucrece,
with which she uses to seal, 'tis my lady. To
whom should this be?

Fabian: This wins him, liver and all.

Malvolio [reads]: "Jove knows, I love:
But who?   87
Lips, do not move;
No man must know."
"No man must know."–What follows?–The
number's altered!–"No man must know."–If this
should be thee, Malvolio?

Sir Toby: Marry, hang thee, brock!   93

Malvolio: "I may command, where I adore:
But silence, like a Lucrece knife,
With bloodless stroke my heart doth gore;
M, O, A, I, doth sway my life."

Fabian: A fustian riddle!   98

Sir Toby: Excellent wench, say I.

Malvolio: "M, O, A, I, doth sway my life."–Nay, but first,
let me see,–let me see,–let me see.

Fabian: What a dish of poison has she dressed him!   101

Sir Toby: And with what wing the staniel checks at it!

Malvolio: "I may command where I adore." Why, she may

command me: I serve her, she is my lady. Why, this is evident to any formal capacity. There is no obstruction in this. And the end—what should that alphabetical position portend? If I could make that resemble something in me,—Softly!— *M, O, A, I.*— 109

Sir Toby: O, ay, make up that! He is now at a cold scent.

Fabian: Sowter will cry upon't for all this, though it be as rank as a fox. 112

Malvolio: *M,*—Malvolio;—*M,*—why, that begins my name.

Fabian: Did not I say that he would work it out? The cur is excellent at faults.

Malvolio: M,—But then there is no consonancy in the sequel; that suffers under probation: *A* should follow, but *O* does.

Fabian: And *O* shall end, I hope. 119

Sir Toby: Ay, or I'll cudgel him, and make him cry, *O.*

Malvolio: And then *I* comes behind.

Fabian: Ay, an you had any eye behind you, you might see more detraction at your heels than fortunes before you. 124

Malvolio: M, O, A, I. This simulation is not as the former: and yet, to crush this a little, it would bow to me, for every one of these letters are in my name. Soft; here follows prose.—

"If this fall into thy hand, revolve. In my stars I am above thee: but be not afraid of greatness. Some are born great, some achieve greatness, and some have greatness thrust upon them. Thy fates open their hands; let thy blood and spirit embrace them. And, to inure thyself to what thou art like to be, cast thy humble slough, and appear fresh. Be opposite with a kinsman, surly with servants: let thy tongue tang arguments of state; put thyself into the trick of singularity. She thus advises thee that sighs for thee. Remember who commended thy yellow stockings; and wished to see thee ever cross-gartered. I say, remember. Go to; thou art made, if thou desirest to be so; if not, let me see thee a steward still, the fellow of servants, and not worthy to touch fortune's fingers. Farewell. She that would alter services with thee. 146

The Fortunate-Unhappy."

Daylight and champain discovers not more. This is open. I will be proud, I will read politic authors, I will baffle Sir Toby, I will wash off gross acquaintance, I will be point-devise, the very man. I do not now fool myself to let imagination jade me; for every reason excites to this, that my lady loves me. She did commend my yellow stockings of late, she did praise my leg being cross-gartered; and in this she manifests herself to my love, and, with a kind of injunction, drives me to these habits of her liking. I thank my stars I am happy. I will be strange, stout, in yellow stockings, and cross-gartered, even with the swiftness of putting on. Jove, and my stars, be praised!

This scene is a good point from which to make references to other points in the play. It is also a good opportunity to learn how to write in the serious and solemn tone of Malvolio.

REMEMBER In order to get into the role of the character you must remember their actions in other parts of the play.

Write down the other main incidents involving Toby, Maria and Andrew that might be in Malvolio's mind as he approaches the garden. What would he be thinking about these characters and their behaviour? What would he be thinking about the mood of Lady Olivia? Finally, remember that Malvolio is very much aware of his own importance. Would he think of himself as someone who could be of help to Olivia in her time of trouble? Malvolio's opening comments as he strolls in the garden are a help here. Write down the quotations from these comments which match up with the ideas above.

REMEMBER Use the correct tone in your writing, one that will reflect the character's personality and feelings at that point in the play.

(?) *Imagine that you are Malvolio. Write an opening paragraph for a diary of his day. Remember how serious Malvolio is; remember his contempt for others, his envy of their social positions and his desperation to be more than just a servant to Lady Olivia.*

(?) *Now examine Malvolio's reactions to Maria's letter. Notice how Maria plays upon his weaknesses and ambitions. Write the heading 'Weaknesses and Ambitions'. Under this write down the parts of the letter that match these qualities in Malvolio's character.*

Practice

In this scene, Malvolio believes he is close to achieving all his hopes and ambitions. Imagine you are Malvolio. Write a description of how you feel at this point in the play.

You should write about:

- how you are feeling about the other characters before you find the letter

- your feelings for Olivia

- your reaction to the proposals and thoughts in the letter

- what you think will happen in the future.

⊕Directing a scene

Another type of question on the Shakespeare paper will ask you to take the part of the director and write about how you would direct a scene.

This type of question gives you an opportunity to write about the play as a piece of drama for the stage. In your writing you should show that you are aware of the play's dramatic effects.

Look at *Macbeth*, Act IV, Scene 1. At this point in the play, Macbeth has murdered Duncan and Banquo. He goes to meet the witches a second time.

Passage 3: Macbeth

Act IV, Scene 1.

A dark cave. In the middle a cauldron boiling. Thunder.

Enter the three witches.

1 Witch:	Thrice the brinded cat hath mew'd.	
2 Witch:	Thrice; and once the hedge-pig whin'd.	
3 Witch:	Harpier cries:—'Tis time, 'tis time.	
1 Witch:	Round about the caldron go;	
	In the poison'd entrails throw.	5
	Toad, that under cold stone,	
	Days and nights has thirty-one	
	Swelter'd venom sleeping got,	
	Boil thou first i' the charmed pot!	
All:	Double, double, toil and trouble;	10
	Fire burn, and cauldron bubble.	
2 Witch:	Fillet of a fenny snake,	
	In the cauldron boil and bake:	
	Eye of newt, and toe of frog,	
	Wool of bat, and tongue of dog,	15
	Adder's fork, and blind-worm's sting,	
	Lizard's leg, and owlet's wing,	
	For a charm of powerful trouble;	
	Like a hell-broth boil and bubble.	
All:	Double, double, toil and trouble;	20
	Fire burn, and cauldron bubble.	
3 Witch:	Scale of dragon, tooth of wolf;	
	Witches' mummy; maw, and gulf	
	Of the ravin'd salt-sea shark;	
	Root of hemlock digg'd i' the dark;	25
	Liver of blaspheming Jew;	
	Gall of goat, and slips of yew,	

> **! REMEMBER** Ideas on characters and the use of language, supported by appropriate quotations, are equally important in your answer to this type of question.

> **! REMEMBER** There is an obvious opportunity to link the scene with another part of the play: Macbeth's first meeting with the witches, which set him on the path to murder. Having achieved his evil ambition, he returns to them again.

                Sliver'd in the moon's eclipse;
                Nose of Turk, and Tartar's lips;
                Finger of birth-strangled babe,   30
                Ditch-deliver'd by a drab,
                Make the gruel thick and slab;
                Add thereto a tiger's chaudron,
                For the ingredience of our cauldron.

All: Double, double, toil and trouble;   35
                Fire burn, and cauldron bubble.

2 Witch: Cool it with a baboon's blood,
                Then the charm is firm and good.

Enter Hecate.

Hecate: O, well done! I commend your pains;
                And every one shall share i' the gains,   40
                And now about the cauldron sing,
                Like elves and fairies in a ring,
                Enchanting all that you put in.

[Music and a Song, 'Black spirits,' etc. Exit Hecate.]

2 Witch: By the pricking of my thumbs,
                Something wicked this way comes:–   45
                Open, locks, whoever knocks.

Enter Macbeth.

Macbeth: How now, you secret, black, and midnight hags!
                What is't you do?

All: A deed without a name.

Macbeth: I conjure you by that which you profess,   50
                (Howe'er you come to know it,) answer me:
                Though you untie the winds and let them fight
                Against the churches: though the yesty waves
                Confound and swallow navigation up;
                Though bladed corn be lodg'd, and trees
                blown down;   55
                Though castles topple on their warders' heads;
                Though palaces, and pyramids, do slope
                Their heads to their foundations; though the treasure
                Of nature's germens tumble all together,
                Even till destruction sicken, answer me   60
                To what I ask you.

1 Witch: Speak.

2 Witch: Demand.

3 Witch: We'll answer.

1 Witch: Say, if thou'dst rather hear it from our mouths,
        Or from our masters?

Macbeth: Call them, let me see them.

1 Witch: Pour in sow's blood, that hath eaten
        Her nine farrow; grease, that's sweaten   65
        From the murderer's gibbet, throw
        Into the flame.

All: Come, high or low;
        Thyself, and office, deftly show.

Thunder. An Apparition of an armed Head rises.

Macbeth: Tell me, thou unknown power,—

1 Witch: He knows thy thought.
        Hear his speech, but say thou nought.   70

Apparition: Macbeth! Macbeth! Macbeth! Beware Macduff;
        Beware the thane of Fife.—Dismiss me:—Enough.

[Descends.]

Macbeth: Whate'er thou art, for thy good caution, thanks;
        Thou hast harp'd my fear aright:—But one word more:—

1 Witch: He will not be commanded: Here's another,   75
        More potent than the first.

Thunder. An Apparition of a bloody Child rises.

Apparition: Macbeth! Macbeth! Macbeth!—

Macbeth: Had I three ears, I'd hear thee.

Apparition: Be bloody, bold, and resolute; laugh to scorn   79
        The power of man, for none of woman born
        Shall harm Macbeth. *[Descends.]*

Macbeth: Then live, Macduff: what need I fear of thee?
        But yet I'll make assurance double sure,
        And take a bond of fate: thou shalt not live;
        That I may tell pale-hearted fear it lies,   85
        And sleep in spite of thunder.—What is this,

Thunder. An Apparition of a Child crowned, with a Tree in his Hand, rises.

        That rises like the issue of a king;
        And wears upon his baby brow the round
                                And top of sovereignty?

All: Listen, but speak not to't.

Apparition: Be lion-mettled, proud; and take no care
        Who chafes, who frets, or where conspirers are:

                    Macbeth shall never vanquish'd be, until   91
                    Great Birnam wood to high Dunsinane hill
                    Shall come against him. *[Descends.]*

Macbeth: That will never be;
                    Who can impress the forest; bid the tree   95
                    Unfix his earth-bound root? Sweet bodements! good!
                    Rebellion's head, rise never, till the wood
                    Of Birnam rise, and our high-plac'd Macbeth
                    Shall live the lease of nature, pay his breath
                    To time, and mortal custom.–Yet my heart
                    Throbs to know one thing: Tell me, (if your art   101
                    Can tell so much,) shall Banquo's issue ever
                    Reign in this kingdom?

All: Seek to know no more.

Macbeth: I will be satisfied: deny me this,
                    And an eternal curse fall on you! Let me know:–
                    Why sinks that cauldron? and what noise is this?

[Hautboys.]

1 Witch: Show!

2 Witch: Show!

3 Witch: Show!

All: Show his eyes, and grieve his heart;
                    Come like shadows, so depart.   111

*Eight Kings appear, and pass over the Stage in order; the last with
a Glass in his hand; Banquo following.*

Macbeth: Thou art too like the spirit of Banquo; down!
                    Thy crown does sear mine eyeballs:–And thy hair,
                    Thou other gold-bound brow, is like the first:–
                    A third is like the former:–Filthy hags!   115
                    Why do you show me this?–A fourth?–Start, eyes!
                    What! will the line stretch out to the crack of doom?
                    Another yet?–A seventh?–I'll see no more:–
                    And yet the eighth appears, who bears a glass
                    Which shows me many more; and some I see,   120
                    That two-fold balls and treble sceptres carry:
                    Horrible sight!–Now, I see, 'tis true;
                    For the blood-bolter'd Banquo smiles upon me,
                    And points at them for his.–What, is this so?

1 Witch: Ay, sir, all this is so:–But why
                    Stands Macbeth thus amazedly?   126

Come, sisters, cheer we up his sprites,
And show the best of our delights;
I'll charm the air to give a sound,
While you perform your antique round: 130
That this great king may kindly say,
Our duties did his welcome pay.
[Music. The Witches dance, and vanish.]

Macbeth: Where are they? Gone?—Let this pernicious hour
Stand aye accursed in the calendar!—
Come in, without there!

Enter Lennox

Lennox: What's your Grace's will?   135

Macbeth: Saw you the weird sisters?

Lennox: No, my lord.

Macbeth: Came they not by you?

Lennox: No, indeed, my lord.

Macbeth: Infected be the air whereon they ride;
And damn'd all those that trust them!—I did hear   139
The galloping of horse: Who was 't came by?

Lennox: 'Tis two or three, my lord, that bring you word,
Macduff is fled to England.

Macbeth: Fled to England?

Lennox: Ay, my good lord.

Macbeth: Time, thou anticipat'st my dread exploits.
The flighty purpose never is o'ertook,   145
Unless the deed go with it. From this moment,
The very firstlings of my heart shall be
The firstlings of my hand. And even now,
To crown my thoughts with acts, be it thought and
done: The castle of Macduff I will surprise;   150
Seize upon Fife; give to the edge o' the sword
His wife, his babes, and all unfortunate souls
That trace him in his line. No boasting like a fool;
This deed I'll do before this purpose cool.
But no more sights!—Where are these gentlemen?   155
Come, bring me where they are. *[Exeunt.]*

Things a director must think about

■ the dramatic effect of the witches upon the audience. Witches are always associated with evil. How can this quality be emphasised on the stage?

■ think how you would want the witches to speak. Look at the rhythm of

REMEMBER
You need to remember that this is a play. Think about the stage, the way the words are spoken and the effect on the audience.

REMEMBER
When answering a question about directing, you still need to think about aspects of more traditional questions, for example, the feelings of the characters. You must support your ideas with appropriate quotations from the play.

the verse. Could it be performed as chanting – or another menacing style?

■ the words of the third witch in lines 22-34. Should all the words connected with harshness and cruelty be emphasised by the actor?

■ look at the entrance of Macbeth. Think about his appearance on the stage. How should he say those opening words?

■ the apparitions (lines 67–124). How can their appearance be staged to have a dramatic effect on the audience? How would you advise the actor to respond to each of them? You will need to think about Macbeth's position on the stage as well as the particular lines he emphasises in his speeches.

■ look at Macbeth's reaction to the appearance of Banquo. Look at Macbeth's words between lines 112 and 124. A huge range of feeling is expressed here – horror, rage, depression and despair. Match these feelings with words from the speech. This will help you to direct the actor who is playing the part.

■ Look at Macbeth's final speech in the scene. How could you direct the actor to convey to the audience the horror expressed in the final lines?

These points emphasise the various aspects of directing a scene – what it will look like on stage, how the actors will say their lines, being aware of how the audience will be affected and how the scene relates to actions in other parts of the play. You will need to include all these points to write a full answer.

Answers

Many of the questions in this book ask for your own reaction to or opinion of pieces of writing, or to write something original yourself. Obviously, no answer to these can be given here, but if you think about the texts in the ways suggested in the book, or write your work according to what you have learned in the section, your answer should be satisfactory. In the Practice questions, if you refer back to the text and the section that comes before, and respond to all the bullet points, this will guide you to the kind of answer you need.

Some questions relate more directly to aspects of the text. For these, some idea of the elements that should be in your answer are given here. These are only notes and suggestions, however. They are not full answers, as would be expected in the Tests.

Reading leaflets
p.6 Factual writing/writing that plays on your feelings: you'll probably find more factual writing than persuasive writing in this leaflet. This could be because it is from an official organisation (HEA), trying to promote a serious campaign , not directly from a company trying only to make money from its product.
p.8 Design aspects that make the leaflet more appealing: use of colour; different sizes of type; text broken up into small paragraphs.
How pictures persuade: e.g. picture of 5 circles reinforces 5 points of text giving HEA advice next to it. Picture of carrying pouch and applying cream make it look practical and convenient; picture of 2 bottles of cream and carry pouch show you what good value you are getting.

Reading prose
p.10 Fact-based information e.g. it had a fine Norman cathedral; there was a sign outside announcing the cost and the renovations project; there were stout pillars and wooden pews etc. Phrases that show how author sees Durham e.g. a mountain of reddish- brown stone standing high above a lazy green loop in the River Wear; nothing at all to detract from the unutterable soaring majesty of the interior; sumptuously grooved patterns etc.
p.11 Persuasive language e.g. perfect little city; it's wonderful; its glory; modest collection boxes; no nagging for money; unutterable soaring majesty; show of friendliness etc.